CALM

NOISE

CALM the NOISE

Why Adults Must Escape Digital Addiction to Save the Next Generation

NIDHI GUPTA, MD

Published by Best Seller Publishing®, St. Augustine, FL
Best Seller Publishing® is a registered trademark.
Printed in the United States of America.

ISBN: 978-1-969338-96-0

This publication is designed to provide accurate and authoritative information with regard to the subject matter covered. It is sold with the understanding that the publisher is not engaged in rendering legal, accounting, or other professional advice. If legal advice or other expert assistance is required, the services of a competent professional should be sought. The opinions expressed by the author in this book are not endorsed by Best Seller Publishing® and are the sole responsibility of the author rendering the opinion.

For more information, please write:
Best Seller Publishing®
1775 US-1 #1070
St. Augustine, FL 32084
or call 1 (626) 765-9750
Visit us online at: www.BestSellerPublishing.org

Table of Contents

Disclaimer

Calm the Noise is intended for informational and educational purposes only. It is not a substitute for professional medical, mental health, or therapeutic advice. The content represents the author's personal views and understanding of social media, the brain, and addiction. Readers are encouraged to consult qualified professionals for specific medical or mental health concerns. The author and publisher disclaim any liability arising from the use or application of the information contained in this book.

Acknowledgments

Calm the Noise is dedicated to my loving family who not only inspire me but let me practice what I preach. Trust me, it's no easy task raising kids without screens, resisting the lure of giving them iPads during flights, vacations, and social gatherings, turning off my own screens at least 30 minutes before bed, and not accessing emails on my phone. It takes more than just conviction and resolve—it takes teamwork. My family deserves special thanks for sharing this commitment to a screen-conscious lifestyle.

To my parents, whose discipline, self-control, and moderation were not just life lessons—they were survival kits. Growing up, I had no idea how invaluable these traits would become in an era of dopamine-loaded distractions.

To my publishers, Rob Kosberg and Bob Harpole at Best Seller Publishing, for turning a nebulous idea into a tangible reality. You allowed me to imagine not just publishing this book but making an impact. Thank you for keeping me on track when deadlines loomed and for the encouraging words that reminded me why this work is important. As Bob recently emailed me, "I am amazed at the number of stories I am seeing on the news about your subject. We have to get your book out there!"

To my editors at Medical Journal Editors and Best Seller Publishing for polishing the rough edges and ensuring that my ideas came across clearly and powerfully. Your expertise turned my passionate ramblings into a cohesive narrative.

To the loving audience who participated in our digital wellness seminars, workshops, and retreats—you made *Calm the Noise* richer. Your challenging questions, stories, and willingness to explore change added depth to each chapter.

To my patients whose stories taught me more about digital wellness than any textbook ever could. Thank you for trusting me enough to share your journeys in these pages. You remind me of the privilege and responsibility I have in this work.

To my leadership coach, Giovanni Gonzalez, who lit a fire under my vision for Phreedom Foundation and helped me grow it into the movement it is today. You helped me dream bigger and execute better.

To my communications coach, Tara Heaton, for imparting the art of storytelling—an influence that is woven throughout this book.

To my illustrators at Imbibe Technologies India, who took my crude stick figures and turned them into vibrant, engaging illustrations. Thank you for breathing life into the visual storytelling of *Calm the Noise*.

Finally, to Rachel Sheriff, our Marketing and Communications Director at Phreedom Foundation. Thanks for being the calm anchor and for nurturing our shared mission of empowering lives, one family and one screen at a time.

Here's to a world where technology enriches rather than engulfs, where every moment counts, and where connection happens in real life, not just online.

Endorsements

Dr. Nidhi Gupta's *Calm the Noise* is a much-needed guide for our hyper-connected world. If you have ever struggled with balancing time with loved ones while building a meaningful career, you know the silent battle against digital distractions. In a world where our devices pull us in countless directions, this book serves as an essential ally in reclaiming our focus, presence, and well-being.

With profound insight and unwavering leadership, Dr. Gupta not only reveals the hidden costs of digital overstimulation but also embodies the very transformation she champions. Her work is a testament to the power of reclaiming our attention— not just for ourselves, but for the next generation.

More than a book, *Calm the Noise* is a call to action. It empowers us to restore balance, protect our consciousness, and ensure technology enriches rather than enslaves. Dr. Gupta stands as a beacon of hope, guiding us toward a future of deeper connection and true presence.

—**Giovanni Gonzalez**
Transformational Leadership Strategist

Parents everywhere are getting smart to screen time. We understand, in a general sense, that screen time is bad for kids, but questions remain. How do we raise successful, happy children in a screen-filled world? Dr. Nidhi Gupta is a voice of reason in the chaos, providing evidence-backed, easily implemented guidance to families. *Calm the Noise* is a must-read guidebook for those who are looking to prioritize healthy connections and peace.

—Nicki Reisberg

Podcast Host & Digital Safety Advocate,
Scrolling 2 Death Podcast

When it comes to digital distractions, we often aim our focus on children. But Dr. Gupta clearly resets the frame on the intergenerational challenge at hand where adults must take a good look in the mirror and recognize how disrupted and fractured our own attention has become. Through her in-depth understanding and clinical expertise, she lays out actionable solutions that any willing and brave soul can use to reverse device dependence and addiction. With Dr. Gupta's help, our spent minds can find peace and learn to focus on what truly matters.

—Sarah Siegand

Co-founder, Parents Who Fight

Calm the Noise is not about abandoning technology but about using it with intention. In an age where screens dominate our attention, Dr. Nidhi Gupta offers a practical road map to reclaim focus, foster genuine human connections, and create healthier digital habits—at home, work, and beyond.

Whether you are a parent, professional, or someone seeking a more balanced life, this book provides the tools to break free from digital dependency and rediscover what truly matters.

Through research-backed insights, personal anecdotes, and actionable strategies, *Calm the Noise* explores why we are so addicted to screens, who are most at risk, and how digital overuse impacts mental health, productivity, and even road safety. It also reveals the hidden forces that keep us tethered to our devices and how to regain control.

Dr. Nidhi Gupta, a physician and digital wellness expert, brings a wealth of knowledge and experience to this urgent topic. With a passion for helping individuals and families build healthier relationships with technology, she empowers readers to step back from digital overload and embrace a life of greater presence, purpose, and connection.

—Stephen Krempl
International Keynote Speaker,
Corporate Communications Coach, Bestselling Author

Calm the Noise is that rare book that makes you want to shout from a megaphone, "Please read! It will transform your life!" The author, Dr. Nidhi Gupta, has given the world a compact, engaging road map to freedom. It's an eye-opening guide that weaves together well-crafted stories with empirical data to help us take back our lives. Not only does Dr. Gupta clarify the consequences of overindulging in screen time, but she helps outline a strategy that is reasonable and achievable. *Calm the Noise* presents fascinating insights that help us reclaim peace while modeling a foundation that will free the next generation from the dangers of screen addiction.

—Tara Heaton
Bestselling Author, Speaker,
Founder, En Pointe Communication

Calm the Noise isn't just a book—it's a wake-up call. In my clinical practice, an 18-year-old patient casually admitted to spending five hours a day on her phone. When I expressed surprise, she shrugged: *"That's normal."* That's when it hit me—what's *normal* today might actually be alarming.

Are we all just highly evolved thumbs attached to a screen? This modern dilemma is exactly what Dr. Nidhi Gupta unpacks in *Calm the Noise*—an eye-opening, refreshingly practical guide to digital wellness. From the moment I picked it up, I was hooked (ironically, in a way that benefits my brain). Dr. Gupta masterfully explains how WMDs *(Weapons of Mass Distraction)* hijack our attention and well-being—and, more importantly, how to break free. This book is for all ages—we all could use a little help putting our phones down.

—**Nikhil Gupta, M.D., M.P.H.**
Endocrinologist, life360MD.com

How to Use This Book

We are drowning in information,
while starving for wisdom.
—E. O. Wilson

My exploration of digital wellness began in 2014 when some unusual personal and professional observations led me to question the deep, passionate, intimate, and co-dependent *relationship* that I saw forming between humans and technology. I sought answers from the internet, but the more I learned, the more I realized that there was something questionable about our newfound love affair with the piece of metal and plastic that we insisted on always keeping close. It became clear that this novel technology was more than just a way to connect with others. Surprisingly, even though we had the means to be more connected than ever before, we seemed to be feeling more and more disconnected from each other.

Throughout this book, you will see me refer to these gadgets as wireless mobile devices (WMDs): portable gadgets (mobile) that use wireless networks (the internet) to send and receive data. These gadgets include, but are not limited to, smartphones, smartwatches, tablets, iPads, laptops, virtual reality glasses, modern smart television, and video games. Although this acronym (WMD) might raise a few eyebrows (especially among folks in the military), I stand by it. While these devices are not weapons of mass destruction, to me, they are *weapons of mass DISTRACTION.*

I wanted to understand more about this seeming paradox. I began with an in-depth study of the medical literature, devouring over 600 research articles on the subject, and more than 300 online blogs.[1,2] At that time, very few non-fiction books had been written on this subject. Remember, this was in the mid-2010s when WMDs were not as ubiquitous as they are now. I identified a significant spike in related publications between 2015 and 2024, emerging a few years after the introduction of Apple's first iPhone on January 9, 2007—a milestone that inarguably reshaped our relationship with technology.

> **While these devices are not weapons of mass destruction, to me, they are *weapons of mass DISTRACTION.***

In 2019, I launched Phreedom Foundation *(Ungrip Devices. Grip Life)*, a non-profit, 501(c)(3) organization with a mission to empower lives, one family and one screen at a time. The term *Phreedom* is a playful twist on the words *phone* and *freedom*. However, the Phreedom Foundation is about more than just reducing screen time; it's about reclaiming a life of purpose, forging authentic connections, and nurturing the bonds that truly matter.

Let me clarify what I mean by screen time throughout this book. Screen time refers to the discretionary use of screens for entertainment, distraction, or passive leisure; optional stuff such as scrolling, streaming and gaming. I am not referring to time spent working, studying or doing something truly necessary on a screen.

We began by organizing seminars, webinars, workshops, retreats, and even technology-free dining events. Later, I started a successful podcast, *Inspinar* (Inspirational Seminar), and began offering digital wellness coaching for families and individuals. Today, I teach digital wellness at schools, colleges, parent nights, businesses, mental health conferences, corporate events, and community education programs worldwide, both online and in person.

Calm the Noise is your introduction to digital wellness. It is written for anyone looking to understand this new intergenerational challenge and learn how to live in peace with it. Our minds are constantly inundated with notifications, emails, news, social media feeds, dings, buzzes, chimes, endless bits of information—or maybe *noise*? In our pursuit to stay informed and connected, we have lost our sense of what information needs to be retained and what might be purged. Our minds are overloaded, overwhelmed, and stretched thin, leaving little room for what truly matters.

By the end of this book, you will have a solid foundation for differentiating *noise* from information worth retaining. This groundwork will help you begin or continue your own digital wellness practices, positively influencing your family, relationships, work, health, and life.

WHAT YOU WILL FIND IN THIS BOOK

Calm the Noise is divided into five parts, each of which will help you gain a basic understanding of a different aspect of digital wellness. You will also find certain concepts intentionally repeated throughout the book to reinforce their importance.

Part 1 is an introduction to digital wellness. I will outline the fundamental concepts including the trigger loop of WMDs and strategies that can be used to break it.

Part 2 focuses on the psychological and neurochemical pathways that trigger our conditioned responses to WMDs. You will need to understand these concepts to help you identify your own triggers and come up with solutions that work best for you.

Part 3 covers the possibility of *digital addiction* and how to determine where you are on the spectrum of digital wellness.

Part 4 explores the impact of the overuse of WMDs on physical and mental health, productivity, burnout, and distracted driving.

Finally, Part 5 contains my outline of core strategies that will help you achieve digital wellness at home and in the workplace.

Because of the way it is structured, newcomers to digital wellness will get the most out of this book by reading it in order, from start to finish. However, you can also use it as a reference book. If there is a specific topic that interests you, you can find it in the index and jump straight to those pages. The concepts discussed in this book have benefited thousands of individuals and families all over the world and inspired many real-life stories, some of which I have shared in these pages. Although some of these concepts may seem a bit abstract, I hope that the stories I share will demonstrate how these ideas can manifest themselves in your everyday life.

Each chapter in *Calm the Noise* concludes with a section entitled **"Your Actionable Recap,"** which reinforces the concepts reviewed. This is followed by a practical question-and-answer section that addresses concerns such as **"Yes, but ... What if ... How about ...?"**. These questions reflect inquiries that I have received when I teach in-person workshops or online seminars on digital wellness. I have made every effort to abbreviate the questions without losing their essence.

Throughout the book, you will find figures, tables, and cartoons that will strengthen your understanding of these concepts. The cartoons depict real-life stories described in the chapter and serve as quick reference tools for when you are applying these ideas to your life. The dialogues in the cartoons reflect how I talk to my brain in given situations. These of course might vary from your internal conversations. The idea is to verbalize the brain chatter and bring it out to a conscious level so that the narrative can then be changed intentionally.

WHO SHOULD READ THIS BOOK?

If someone wrote a book called *Digital Wellness for Children*, there would be little doubt as to who would read it and with what goal in mind: parents or school leaders aiming to facilitate their children's digital wellness, or children and adolescents themselves, nudged by their parents to read it. However, the concepts underlying digital wellness are quite broad. There are distinct differences (and similarities) in how I approach this subject for children versus adults. Put simply, if parents prioritize healthy habits (for example, healthy eating and physical activity), their children are likely to follow suit. The same is true for digital wellness.

Adult minds (and not just children's) have been rewired by technology. This has made it challenging for adults to separate themselves from their WMDs even momentarily, whether it is during driving, working, vacationing, sleeping, eating, or even showering. Justifying the use of these devices for *work* may be acceptable to a certain degree, but WMD use is frequently uncontrolled.

Unintentionally, parents may be projecting the anxieties that they feel when separated from WMDs onto their children, who then respond accordingly. Therefore, *I believe that adults must escape digital addiction first to save the next generation.*

> Therefore, *I believe that adults must escape digital addiction first to save the next generation.*

Although I began this work by studying research articles about children and their screen time, it became apparent to me that adults' digital wellness was just as crucial, if not more so. Children often become the collateral damage of adults' inability to grasp the impact of digital addiction on their own minds and bodies. While I will do my best to give a broad overview of digital wellness and include topics that will be suitable for all ages, I realize that I am inevitably influenced by the school of thought that posits that first, digital wellness is not about children only, and second, children are not the key decision-makers in how and when they are introduced to WMDs. My hope is that you will gain an in-depth understanding of digital wellness concepts and solutions to digital addiction, and apply these ideas to your life to uplift yourself and those around you.

DETOX AND CONNECTION

In the digital wellness space, we often hear the words *detox* and *connected*. Detox in this case means a desire or process that can be used to calm the perceived over-exhaustion that results from being persistently accessible. Connected refers to the need to be persistently accessible and to remain aware of everything going on at all times. Detox traditionally translates to a process used to help people stop using harmful substances or putting unhealthy foods and drinks into their bodies to improve their health and well-being.

True digital wellness emphasizes that you can use your own methods and techniques on the path to digital detox while staying connected in a way that feels nurturing but not harmful to you. The teachings in this book can be adapted by each reader based on the perceived need to detox while staying connected.

Now let's begin exploring digital wellness together!

Part 1
Getting Grounded

1
The Story of My Own Digital (Un)Wellness

Technology is a useful servant but a dangerous master.
—Christian Lous Lange (1869–1938)

It was nearly 2:00 p.m. I had just finished a marathon clinic day. I was running on fumes. I knew I had about 20 patient charts to document, five prescriptions to send to the pharmacy, and a whopping 27 emails begging for my attention. Just staring at the number of tasks looming over my desk made me queasy. To add a little more chaos, my *very smart* cell phone glowed, reminding me to pick up my kids from school by 3:10 p.m. I had an entire golden hour to spare—60 minutes of pure, unadulterated potential ... or so I thought.

Then, like clockwork, I heard a mischievous voice in my head (I have since named it *the devil on standby*): "Hey, you have earned a break, doctor! You have toiled enough. How about a quick peek at those adorable videos of your kids?" It seemed harmless enough. So, I took the bait and dove right down the rabbit hole of family memories. There they were, my munchkins frolicking on the beach, creating chaos with sand and water, and collecting seashells like they were precious gems. Every moment was meticulously captured on video or photo because, let's be honest, who needs to live in the present when you have a smartphone?

As I basked in the warm glow of nostalgia, time slipped away. My mind, now in vacation mode, demanded an encore. Back then, I did not realize what my brain was craving. It was like a siren song of bliss, luring me away from my responsibilities. It whispered sweet nothings like, "Just a few more minutes of 'me time,' then you will be able to tackle that mountain of work with more energy." And so, I gave in. I tapped open a social media app, and what happened next? I'm sure you know exactly what happened.

When I finally tore my eyes away from the digital abyss, I was startled—it was already 3:10 p.m.! My poor little kids were probably baking in the afternoon sun, scanning the horizon for a white Honda Odyssey that had not yet appeared. I could already picture their disappointed faces at being the last ones to be picked up, wondering if their mom had forgotten all about them.

Was it worth it? Were those 60 minutes of entertainment, digital self-indulgence, *me time, relaxation, taking a break*, or whatever else I could use to justify it, worth the impending chaos?

Was it worth it? Were those 60 minutes of entertainment, digital self-indulgence, *me time, relaxation, taking a break,* or whatever else I could use to justify it, worth the impending chaos?

Why did my mind play tricks on me? Why did it make me *want* to continue watching the digital content? Why did it not knock some sense into my wandering thoughts and direct my attention to what needed to be done? After all, I wasn't getting paid to have fun at work! Whose fault was it anyway? Mine? My smartphone's? The mischievous devil on standby? Or perhaps a bit of all three?

What could I have done differently with those precious 60 minutes? Would life be any different if I did not always have a pocket-sized computer with me 24/7? Would that have saved me some time? But then again, how would I survive without my trusty sidekick? My smartphone was my one-stop shop for time, stopwatch, alarm clock, chatting, news, calendar, calculator, emails, notes, reminders, banking, health, travel, grocery, entertainment, podcasts, music, weather, social media, and of course telephone calls—although that seemed like the least-used function on it. How could I blame my smartphone for my own need to rely on it and outsource all these functions to it?

The one-stop shop

Considering everything that my smartphone obediently did for me, even imagining that there was something suspicious about it, was of course laughable. Even if it was doing something suspicious to my mind, I was not going to give it up. Of course not! What if there was an urgent email or a pressing patient need? How could I be so irresponsible as to ignore that? What would I do with myself while waiting in the checkout line at the grocery store?

How would I do my job? I would lose business if I did not reply fast enough. How would I keep tabs on everything happening halfway across the world (whether it was relevant to me or not)? How could I miss out on happenings in other people's lives on social media?

The fear was real ... the dreaded fear of missing out (otherwise known as FOMO). The fear of being left out, not belonging, being the weird one. I could practically feel the FOMO-induced shivers running down my spine, and beads of sweat forming on my forehead.

As I gathered my unfinished tasks, stuffing the paperwork into my bag, a sinking feeling settled in. Tonight, after the kids were tucked into bed, I would be facing a marathon of catch-up work—all because I could not resist the siren call of digital distractions.

Little did I know, these seemingly innocuous incidents were just symptoms of a much larger problem. They sparked a curiosity in me, leading me to explore current research focused on the impact of new technologies on the human mind. What I discovered was startling: Workplace distractions, especially those caused by digital devices, have recently emerged as a significant concern in the scientific literature. For example, Gloria Mark and her colleagues at the University of California, Irvine, found that it takes an average of 19–25 minutes to regain focus after a single distraction.[3] Imagine that—nearly half an hour lost each time your attention is diverted by a notification or a quick glance at social media. Similarly, a survey conducted by online learning and teaching marketplace, Udemy, revealed that 70 percent of employees feel distracted at work, with digital devices identified as the primary culprits.[4] Alarmingly, employees also acknowledged that 45–80 percent of their distractions stem from using technology for personal activities, primarily checking social media. I guess I was not alone in this struggle.

As a part of my efforts to build good habits and break bad ones, I came across an idea in James Clear's book *Atomic Habits:* Habits are, simply, reliable solutions to recurring problems in our environment.[5] James Clear, and previously, Charles Duhigg, broke down the process of building a habit into four simple steps: cue, craving, response, and reward. My intention is to integrate these steps into our understanding of the relationship that we have formed with our wireless mobile devices (WMDs). I give full recognition to authors Charles Duhigg, Nir Eyal, and James Clear for their varied representations and designs of the habit loop. In the context of WMD usage, I have retitled this idea as *the trigger loop of WMDs.*

To regain control over our digital habits, we need to understand what drives them. Our relationship with WMDs follows a predictable loop—one that can be broken if we recognize its components.

First, there is the cue, which in my story was fatigue after a long day at work and the noisy feeling that *I deserved a break.* The cue triggered my brain to initiate a craving that might eventually lead to a reward. The craving was not for the photos of my kids, but for the change that this experience delivers. The craving led to the response of grabbing my phone and browsing. Finally, the response delivered a reward, that is, *it satisfied my craving.* At least for a moment, the reward delivered contentment and relief from the craving (until the next cue came along). Honestly, if I did not have to pick up my kids from school, I could have been scrolling for hours.

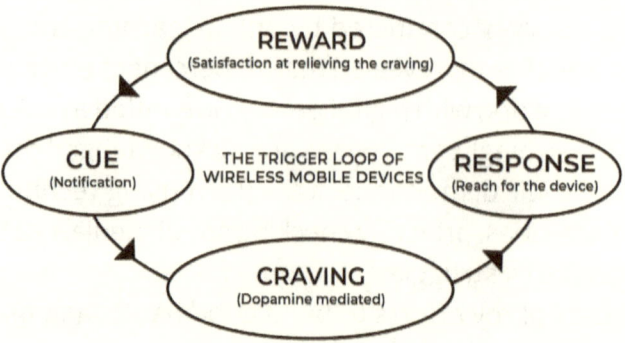

The trigger loop of WMDs

If the trigger loop is interrupted at any of the aforementioned four steps, it will not become a habit. Delete the cues and the craving would never manifest. Curb the craving and the motivation to respond will be reduced. Weaken the response and you will be unable to collect the reward. Dull the reward and make it less satisfying, or make the alternative more satisfying, and then you will have no reason to repeat the trigger loop. In the chapters that follow, we will discuss the trigger loop in more detail. I will show you strategies that you can use to break the trigger loop so that you can create a system in which your WMDs serve you as tools instead of 24/7 sources of distraction and entertainment.

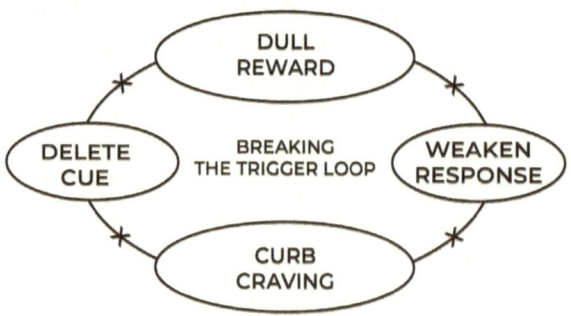

Breaking the trigger loop of WMDs

As I sit here penning the first few chapters of this book, I am still tethered to my trusty smartphone. But something has changed. My smartphone now dutifully serves as a tool, and not as my 24/7 source of distraction and entertainment. Also, I no longer refer to my phone as *smart.* That would imply it's

My smartphone now dutifully serves as a tool, and not as my 24/7 source of distraction and entertainment.

the one running the show, which frankly, is giving it way too much credit. Instead, I have downgraded it to a *wireless mobile device*, or as I fondly call it in my native Hindi language, the *duurbhaash* (literally, talking from afar). Because that's what it was originally designed for, right?

Looking back, I realize that my struggles were not unique. So many of us wrestle with the same issues, losing hours to mindless scrolling, feeling constantly distracted, and wondering why we can't just put our WMDs down. Before I embarked on this literary journey (of note, the first draft was scribbled across 70 pages of a 10.5-inch × 8-inch notebook, because apparently, I am a glutton for punishment), I took a bold step. I powered down my WMD, stashed it out of sight, and tried my darnedest to forget about it. It was out of sight ... although unfortunately, never out of mind.

CALM THE NOISE AT YOUR WORKPLACE

DELETE THE CUES

Instead of

*Turn off
non-essential notifications*

CURB THE CRAVING

Instead of

Stretch, Blink, Hydrate

WEAKEN THE RESPONSE

Instead of

Tuck WMD away

DULL THE REWARD

Instead of

*Find joy in
reclaiming your time*

Your Actionable Recap

- WMDs serve as *weapons of mass distraction.*
- It takes an average of 19–25 minutes to regain focus after a distraction.
- Outsourcing multiple simple needs to the WMDs increases our dependency on and attachment to them.
- FOMO is real and needs to be acknowledged in this conversation.
- We are in this together. Just because I have the privilege of writing this book does not make me a hero in the fight against digital distractions.

Yes, but ... What if ... How about?

- **Yes, but how did you manage to balance your responsibilities and resist digital distractions in the long term?**
  Finding balance is an ongoing journey, not a destination. I did not overcome digital distractions overnight and cannot claim to have mastered them entirely, even now. I realized that this journey requires a combination of self-awareness, discipline, consistency, and practical strategies that we will explore in the following chapters. You will learn more about the trigger loop and how to break it, as well as how to recondition your mindset from *escape-displace* to *engage-replace.* By understanding these concepts, you might find it easier to resist distractions and discover more time for your offline life.

- **What if you had not succumbed to the distractions that day? How might your work and personal life have been different?**
  If I had managed to resist the pull of digital distractions that day, I would have likely thought of alternative ways to take a break—sip water, blink a few times, stretch, and talk to a friend or colleague. I might have completed my tasks efficiently and enjoyed a more relaxed evening with my children. For me, those moments of distraction served as a wake-up call. They highlighted the need for change and underscored the fact that digital distraction is as much an issue for adults as it is for children.

- **How about other tools or methods beyond just powering down your WMD? Did you find any additional techniques or practices that helped you regain control?**
  Powering down my WMD was just the first step in regaining control over my time and my life. As I progressed, I discovered several other tools and practices that were crucial in maintaining focus and resisting the lure of constant connectivity. Uncluttering and triaging the contents of my WMDs, along with turning off non-essential notifications, freed up so much mental space that the idea of writing this book finally took root!

2
What Is Digital Wellness?

We expect more from technology and less from each other.
—**Sherry Turkle**

As I boarded my flight to San Diego, I was dismayed, shocked, and saddened to see nearly every head—adult and child—bent over a wireless mobile device (WMD). I noticed a family of five—three siblings and their parents—sitting next to each other, yet utterly disconnected from one another, each lost in the pursuits of the virtual world as the real world passed by.

Fingers flew across different social media feeds faster than the airplane itself. Passengers caught rapid-fast snippets of a soccer game, furiously typed last-minute text messages, frantically tried to download a movie while cursing the poor Wi-Fi connection, and hurriedly settled their little ones in front of heavily padded iPads. The deep, incessant need to be *prepared* before the flight attendant's inevitable command to switch WMDs to airplane mode was palpable, along with the ensuing fear of that deep, dark black hole of the world without internet access.

I settled into my middle seat, flanked on one side by a young woman in her mid-20s and on the other by a man in his mid-60s. As I pulled out my notebook to continue writing, I was acutely aware of the curious—perhaps even scandalized—gazes of my co-passengers.

The hurried, almost frantic behavior exhibited by the passengers just before take-off may reflect more than just a desire to stay occupied. It may be a sign of a subtle anxiety induced by the thought of being without the internet for a few hours, or a subconscious fear of being bored. Nicholas Carr, in his book *The Shallows: What the Internet Is Doing to Our Brains,* discusses how our constant connectivity rewires our brains, leading to shorter attention spans and a diminished capacity for deep thinking.[6] Similarly, Maggie Jackson, in her book *Distracted: Reclaiming Our Focus in a World of Lost Attention,* argues that our society's obsession with multitasking and instant gratification is eroding our ability to focus and engage in meaningful activities.[7]

The passengers' behavior—rapidly scrolling through social media feeds, trying to catch up on everything that has happened—might also stem from the fear of missing out (FOMO). There is an underlying belief that if we do not stay constantly connected, we might fall behind, missing something crucial or life-changing.

For parents, the priority of placing their young ones in front of their WMDs seems to outweigh even stowing away luggage in the overhead bin. Is this done to prevent the children from disturbing other travelers, or is it more about allowing the parents to immerse themselves in their own (de)vices? Meanwhile, the other passengers are already cozily transported to their own virtual heavens, seemingly indifferent to any disruptions from the children around them. So, let's be honest, who would simply sit in silence on a flight today?

One might argue, what is the harm in all of this? After all, there is nothing else to do on a flight anyway. This is partly true, and it touches on a key point of digital wellness. We have surrounded ourselves with an endless barrage of information sources, yet we have lost sight of what it feels like to not be constantly bombarded with bits and bytes of data—much of which is trivial, outright misinformation, or *noise*.[8]

The constant inflow of digital noise keeps the mind full, stimulated, active, engaged, busy, captivated, entertained ... or more accurately, *spent*. The mind has no time to rest or reset. It is trapped in a hyper-stimulated state that eventually becomes the new way of being; the new normal. This state of constant stimulation (perhaps even feeling *high*) is addictive and leaves the mind resistant to any other state. Anything else feels boring, daunting, uncomfortable, irritating, anxiety-provoking, and *abnormal*.

> **We have surrounded ourselves with an endless barrage of information sources, yet we have lost sight of what it feels like to not be constantly bombarded with bits and bytes of data.**

The human mind has an incredible capacity to process information. Yet even the fastest processors in the world can get *frozen* or *hung up* if tasked with downloading an excessively large file or infiltrated with too many clicks in rapid succession. Similarly, once the mind's threshold for data intake is reached, it begins to shut down. Additional stimuli only serve to overwhelm an already overloaded system, leading to mental fatigue and burnout.

Imagine a scenario on this flight: Exhausted parents (including me), their systems already digitally overloaded from endless notifications, social media updates, and work emails, find themselves snapping at their child who is throwing a tantrum to get their attention. The child's cries are not just another noise—they are the final straw in a mind that has been stretched to its limit. The parents, drained and overwhelmed, respond with frustration rather than the patience their child desperately needs. It's a moment that highlights how digital overload can rob us of our ability to cope with life's everyday challenges, leading to stress and strained relationships.

This phenomenon is not just anecdotal; it's backed by research. A study published in *The Journal of the Association for Consumer Research* found that the mere presence of a smartphone, even when not in use, can reduce available cognitive capacity and impair performance on tasks requiring attention. The study's authors concluded that our smartphones could serve as a type of *brain drain*, detracting from our ability to concentrate, think deeply, and make decisions effectively.[9]

Digital wellness, then, is not merely about reducing screen time; it's about reclaiming control over our cognitive resources, our time, and ultimately, our lives. It's about recognizing that being constantly *on* does not equate to being productive or fulfilled. In fact, this state often has the opposite effect, leading to a life where we are always connected yet increasingly disconnected from ourselves and those around us.

As I continued to fill the pages of my notebook, I noticed a growing sense of uneasiness in my mid-60s co-passenger.

Digital wellness, then, is not merely about reducing screen time; it's about reclaiming control over our cognitive resources, our time, and ultimately, our lives.

His restlessness was obvious, and I could feel his gaze occasionally drifting toward my notes. Sensing his discomfort, I looked up from my writing and offered him a warm smile. That simple gesture was all it took for him to start sharing his life story—a tale marked by ongoing struggles with his adult son's digital addiction. He confessed to having stealthily read over my shoulder.

I gently closed my notebook. The rest of the flight was spent in providing personalized digital wellness coaching to this concerned father. We discussed strategies, shared insights, and explored ways to support his son in reclaiming control over his digital life. As our conversation drew to a close, we exchanged business cards, agreeing to continue the discussion later.

Meanwhile, on my other side, my co-passenger in her mid-20s had invested in the onboard Wi-Fi, her attention fully captured by the WMD she held precariously and, I imagined, somewhat painfully in her hand for the entire four hours of the flight. These patterns of compulsive WMD use are not random. They are deeply ingrained habits reinforced by behavioral/trigger loops.

The message emblazoned across each seat of the airplane—*WATCH NOW!*—seemed to sum up the choices we all face in this hyper-connected age. While one of us was diving deeper into the virtual world, another was seeking a way out for a loved one. I found myself in the middle, bridging the gap between the digital chaos and the quest for wellness.

CALM THE NOISE DURING AIR TRAVEL

DELETE THE CUES

Instead of

Turn off and stow WMD

CURB THE CRAVING

Instead of

Talk, Play, Engage

WEAKEN THE RESPONSE

Instead of

Disconnect from internet

DULL THE REWARD

Instead of

Congratulate yourself on curbing the craving

YOUR ACTIONABLE RECAP

- Constant connectivity rewires our brains, leading to shorter attention spans and a diminished capacity for deep thinking.
- Digital overload can lead to mental fatigue and stress, diminishing our ability to cope with everyday challenges.
- WMDs can serve as a *brain drain*, reducing our ability to concentrate and make decisions effectively.
- Human connection remains crucial, even in a world dominated by screens. Sometimes, all it takes is a smile to open a meaningful conversation.

YES, BUT ... WHAT IF ... HOW ABOUT?

- **Yes, but seriously, what is the harm in watching a movie on a flight?**
  There is nothing inherently wrong with watching a movie or enjoying some entertainment on a flight. Flights can be long and tiring, and we all need ways to pass the time. The concern arises when this habit extends to every unoccupied moment of our lives, creating a cycle of dependency where our mind constantly craves quick hits of information and entertainment. While it's true that there is only so much time one can spend gazing out the window at the fluffy clouds and expansive horizon, it's also crucial to give our minds and eyes a break from the digital noise.

- **What if I need something to kill boredom on a flight?**
  There are plenty of ways to make a flight more enjoyable without relying solely on WMDs. You might consider

bringing along a good book, catching up on some much-needed sleep, or engaging in a conversation with your co-passenger. Sometimes, the best stories come from the person sitting next to you. These activities not only help reboot your system but also offer a change of pace that can be refreshing.

If you are traveling with children, consider packing age-appropriate non-WMD activities such as puzzles, coloring books, or small toys that can keep them entertained while avoiding over-reliance on WMDs. Snacks are always a good idea, too. And remember, it's okay for them to embrace a bit of boredom. Sometimes, letting the mind wander without any particular focus can feel uplifting.

- **How about using WMD-free activities on the plane to keep boredom at bay?**
  WMD-free activities on a plane are a great idea, but they will be far more effective if they are already part of your or your child/family's routine off the plane. Relying on WMD-free time only during a flight while being immersed in WMDs at other times, can lead to withdrawal symptoms, crankiness, and even worse outcomes.

  To make WMD-free activities truly enjoyable and beneficial, it's important to integrate them into daily life well before you board the plane. This way, you and your child will be more comfortable and less reliant on WMDs, whether in the air or on the ground.

3
Understanding the
Trigger Loop

You do not rise to the level of your goals.
You fall to the level of your systems.
—**James Clear,** *Atomic Habits*

On a cozy February evening, a group of 45 female physicians gathered for the winter social of the Tennessee Women in Medicine. A few months earlier, I had delivered a keynote at the organization's annual meeting where we discussed strategies for life-technology balance, especially in the context of balancing motherhood while practicing medicine.

During the evening, one of my colleagues, Dr. Sara Thompson, approached me. "Nidhi," she exclaimed, "my life has changed since I heard your keynote. Look at what I am wearing!" She proudly extended her arm, showing off an analog wristwatch. "Since that talk, I switched from my smartwatch, and it has transformed my life!"

I was both humbled and impressed by her simple yet profound shift. Reflecting on Dr. Thompson's feedback together with that of countless others who have shared similar sentiments after attending our workshops, I began to realize the power of small changes. Sometimes, it takes just a small nudge to create life-changing outcomes.

Throughout this book, I have explored similar tools and strategies to break free from compulsive wireless mobile device (WMD) usage. While you may feel that you have heard these suggestions before, I encourage you to consider them with a fresh perspective and integrate them into your life with the insights you are gaining from this book.

Internet and WMD addiction are emerging fields with no standardized treatment yet. However, approaches like cognitive-behavioral therapy, motivational interviewing, and certain medications show promise. Since WMD addiction and substance addiction affect similar brain pathways, proven treatments for substance abuse may also be effective for WMD addiction.[10]

Complete abstinence from WMDs is not feasible in today's digital world. Moderation and balance are critical components of lifelong digital wellness. Unfortunately, WMD use has been normalized to the point where it can feel nearly impossible to imagine a different way of life for us, our families, and our communities. Constant connectivity, instant replies to texts and emails, and the pressure to always be *on* can create major barriers to changing our habits.

Our behaviors around WMDs are deeply ingrained in trigger loops, reinforced by repeated cues and rewards. Let's revisit the four steps of habit formation that shape the trigger loop of WMDs:

Cue → Craving → Response → Reward

The trigger loop is driven by the brain's reward system, which is regulated by dopamine.[11] Dopamine, often called *the anticipation hormone*, plays a major role in reinforcing addictive behaviors. The anticipation of rewards (e.g., likes, notifications, new content) might trigger dopamine release, creating a *hook* for repetitive behavior.

Over time, WMD overuse can desensitize the dopamine receptors, requiring greater stimulation to achieve the same reward.[12] A loop of increasing use with diminishing returns is formed.

Some individuals with baseline dopamine deficiencies (e.g., in conditions like attention-deficit/hyperactivity disorder (ADHD) or depression) may be more prone to seeking external stimuli to compensate for their underactive reward systems.

While direct research showing that WMD overuse increases dopamine levels in the brain is currently limited,[13] inferences may be drawn from decades of research on behavioral addiction.

Here is how the trigger loop of WMDs may play out:

- **Cue –** A notification, a buzz, the glow of the WMD screen, or simply glancing at a screen may be enough to elicit dopamine release and spark the question: *What did I get?*
- **Craving –** This cue may be followed by the immediate urge or craving to check the WMD to satisfy the need for a reward in the form of new information or connection.
- **Response –** The user might then reach for the WMD, check it, and consume the information.
- **Reward –** A sense of relief or satisfaction might occur once the information has been processed, reinforcing the behavior.

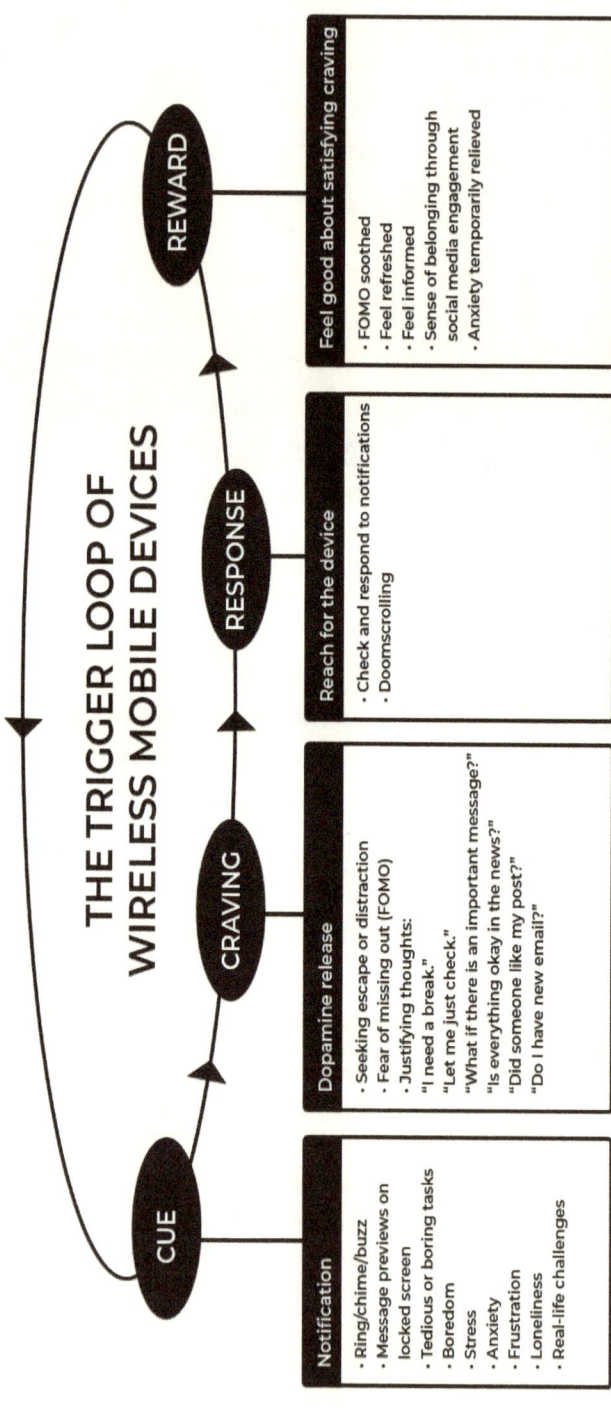

THE TRIGGER LOOP OF
WIRELESS MOBILE DEVICES

CUE → **CRAVING** → **RESPONSE** → **REWARD**

Notification

- Ring/chime/buzz
- Message previews on locked screen
- Tedious or boring tasks
- Boredom
- Stress
- Anxiety
- Frustration
- Loneliness
- Real-life challenges

Dopamine release

- Seeking escape or distraction
- Fear of missing out (FOMO)
- Justifying thoughts:
  "I need a break."
  "Let me just check."
  "What if there is an important message?"
  "Is everything okay in the news?"
  "Did someone like my post?"
  "Do I have new email?"

Reach for the device

- Check and respond to notifications
- Doomscrolling

Feel good about satisfying craving

- FOMO soothed
- Feel refreshed
- Feel informed
- Sense of belonging through social media engagement
- Anxiety temporarily relieved

The trigger loop of WMDs shows how notifications and emotional cues can trigger craving, leading to WMD use and a temporary reward. The short-term relief reinforces the behavior, creating a trigger loop driven by dopamine release. Understanding this loop is the first step toward breaking free from compulsive WMD checking.

When this cycle is repeated multiple times, it may become woven into the fabric of the mind. The ease of access to the internet and its contents via a WMD significantly boost the addictiveness of this behavior pattern. Soon, even without notifications, we habitually reach for our WMDs because we have become trained to expect a reward. This behavior can operate on autopilot, without our conscious awareness.

For example, in Chapter 1, I dreaded the tedious task of documenting clinic notes. The mere thought of starting the task was fraught with discomfort. My mind sought relief and craving followed. I unlocked my WMD, browsed through photos, and felt immediate relief. My dopamine had spiked, rewarding me with fleeting pleasure.

The thought of initiating a tedious task or being bored on the flight becomes associated with browsing the WMD. The result? Habit gets formed. Behavior is shaped. The mind is conditioned. No alternatives seem acceptable. Each cue makes the mind crave a reward. Each reward makes the mind wait eagerly for the next cue. Over time, casual WMD use escalates into dependency and addiction.

WMD use → WMD overuse →
WMD dependency → WMD addiction

This sequence opens the trap of procrastination, loss of sense of time, and the psychological need to check the WMD constantly.

This is exactly how addictive drugs work.[14]

From the moment we wake up, our WMDs serve as a constant source of lip-smacking, pleasure-inducing dopamine drip that keeps us hooked. This digital dopamine drip has become so integral to our lives that many of us cannot even get out of bed without reaching for a quick fix, whether it's checking notifications, scrolling through social media, or watching videos.

The 24/7 dopamine drip

Time	Activity	Associated Justification for Dopamine	What to Do Instead? Calm the Noise!
6:00 AM	Waking up	Check notifications to feel awake and to make sure everything was okay overnight.	• Resist checking WMD for 30 minutes. • Start the day mindfully.
6:30 AM	Getting ready for work	Watch a short video for mood boost.	• Calm any external noise or play soothing music if you must.
7:00 AM	Breakfast	Scroll social media while eating, for entertainment.	• Eat mindfully, savor the food, and connect with those around you.
7:30 AM	Getting ready to leave for work	Check email to be prepared.	• Avoid checking email on WMD. Instead, use a desktop.
8:00 AM	Commuting to work	Scroll emails, messages, and social media to kill commute boredom.	• Listen to an audiobook or playlist while keeping WMD untouched.
8:30 AM	Starting work	Check emails and messages as they come to avoid missing something urgent.	• Set time-blocks for focused work. • Silence non-essential notifications.
12:00 PM	Lunch break	Watch videos or browse apps for stress relief.	• Take a walk outside, hydrate, stretch, or have a screen-free lunch.

Time	Activity	Associated Justification for Dopamine	What to Do Instead? Calm the Noise!
2:00 PM	Afternoon slump	Check social media for engagement and interaction.	• Catch up with a colleague. • Work on an easier task.
5:00 PM	Commuting home	Scroll emails, messages, and social media to kill commute boredom (again) and to stay awake.	• Listen to an audiobook or playlist while keeping WMD untouched.
7:00 PM	Family time	Scroll for mental escape.	• Engage with family, play a game, or share highlights of the day. • Spend outdoor time together.
9:00 PM	Relaxing before bed	Watch short videos or play video games for relaxation and me time.	• Journal, meditate, or read a physical book to wind down. • Prepare for the next day.
10:30 PM	In bed, ready to sleep	Scroll to feel calm before sleeping.	• Leave WMD in another room • Use a traditional alarm clock.

Throughout the day, WMD dependency manifests as compulsive interruptions, pulling us away from tasks, conversations, and moments of focus to seek yet another hit of dopamine. Ironically, we have long judged smokers for stepping away from work for their nicotine breaks, labeling it as disruptive and compulsive. Yet, we have normalized an eerily similar behavior in ourselves, one that doesn't just take us outside for a few minutes but keeps us tethered to our screens for hours.

The parallels are striking and challenge us to reconsider how we have allowed this dependency to infiltrate every aspect of our lives. It is not just about the time spent on our devices or the scattered attention span; it is about what is being displaced as a result.

Our days and time are finite, with limited hours available to meet essential needs like sleep, physical activity, schoolwork, office work, social interactions, hobbies, and personal care. A little leisure screen time isn't inherently harmful, but the problem arises when WMD use *displaces* these essential activities.

> **You cannot even imagine how transformative it is to reclaim your time and attention.**

It is particularly concerning for children. Parents often ask:
How much screen time should be allowed for my child?

But the better question is:
What essential activities are being displaced by screen time?

More on this topic will be presented in later chapters.

This discussion brings us to a critical turning point: What can you do about it?

You cannot even imagine how transformative it is to reclaim your time and attention.

To reclaim control over your time and attention, you must break the trigger loop of WMDs.

The trigger loop—Cue → Craving → Response → Reward—feels inescapable at first, but awareness is the key to breaking free. Once you recognize the pattern and identify the cues, it becomes easier to intervene and disrupt the cycle.

Before we explore key strategies to disrupt the trigger loop in the next chapter, let's bust a common myth: We are addicted to our WMDs.

The WMD itself isn't the real problem. The true addiction lies elsewhere.

The device (WMD) is just the medium. It is merely a tool.
The addiction is not to the device.
The addiction is to the content.
The addiction is to distraction.
The addiction is to the need to avoid boredom.
The addiction is to the feeling of being informed.

Dr. Thompson's decision to switch from a smartwatch to an analog wristwatch was a pivotal moment in her journey toward digital wellness. By removing the constant flood of notifications from her smartwatch, she effectively deleted

> *The addiction is not to the device. The addiction is to the content.*

the primary cue in the trigger loop, breaking the cycle before it could even begin. This simple, yet powerful change allowed her to regain control over her attention and be more present in both her personal and professional life.

Without the constant craving and response that notifications elicit, Dr. Thompson no longer felt the pressure to constantly check her wrist for updates. Her analog watch doesn't just tell her the time; it represents her freedom from the digital distractions that once consumed her.

Breaking the habit of compulsive WMD use doesn't always require monumental changes. Sometimes, it's the simplest decisions that can lead to profound shifts in how we interact with our devices and the world around us.

Your Actionable Recap

- Habits are formed through repetition—each trigger loop reinforces the cycle of distraction.
- The device is not the problem—it's the content, embedded with reward mechanisms, that keeps us hooked.
- We must prioritize essential activities such as sleep, exercise, and face-to-face interactions, before we turn to screens.
- Small and simple changes lead to monumental shifts over time.

Yes, but ... What if ... How about?

- **Yes, but I use my smartwatch to count my steps and monitor my heart rate.**

  That's fantastic! Tracking your fitness goals is a great use of a smartwatch. It's like having a personal trainer on your wrist. However, it's important to reflect on whether your interaction with the smartwatch is limited to these productive uses.

  Ask yourself, *"Am I frequently checking notifications, emails, or messages? Do I find myself looking at my smartwatch even during conversations or meetings?"* If the constant connectivity is leading to feelings of being *always* on or anxiety when you don't have your smartwatch with you, it may indicate that your relationship with the device goes beyond just a fitness tool. After all, fitness should be about freeing your mind too, right?

- **What if I turn off notifications on my WMD and miss something urgent?**
  It is understandable to worry about missing something important, but managing this fear is part of breaking the cycle of dependency on constant connectivity. One way to address this is by taking scheduled breaks from your WMD, and yes, actually *physically* separating from it—leaving it in another room. Let people know that urgent matters can also be communicated through alternative channels, like a landline phone.

  Taking breaks from your WMD for set periods each day allows your mind to reset and can help reduce the stress of always being available.

- **How about switching back to a flip phone?**
  Jose Briones, the creator of *dumbphones.org*, developed a platform to help users find the right *dumb phone* for their needs. In Episode 37 of our podcast *Inspinar*, Jose wisely pointed out that "Switching to a flip phone will not guarantee digital de-addiction—changing your lifestyle will."

  While a flip phone can reduce certain distractions, shifting attention to other screens, such as laptops, iPads, or televisions, may offset any benefits. The key lies in modifying how you engage with technology as a whole, not just the handheld devices you use.

4
Strategies to Break the Trigger Loop

Change might not be fast, and it isn't always easy.
But with time and effort, almost any habit can be reshaped.
—**Charles Duhigg**, *The Power of Habit*

Alison is a 17-year-old young woman whose mother brought her to see me because she was having trouble gaining weight. The family wanted to rule out any hormonal imbalances, so they sought my help as an endocrinologist.

After running all of the necessary tests and reviewing her blood work, I found no endocrine issues.

As it turned out, Alison had received a smartphone at the age of 14. Like many teenagers, she quickly created accounts on multiple social media platforms. Soon after, her behavior began to shift. Alison became more withdrawn, interacting less frequently with her parents. She was irritable when asked about her day, often locking herself in her room. Her parents noticed that she seemed more anxious, perhaps even depressed.

Over the next few years, Alison lost 30 pounds, bringing her down to 98 pounds at a height of 5 feet, 6 inches. She had become hyper-focused on counting calories and began skipping meals altogether. Despite seeing a counselor, psychiatrist, and dietician, nothing seemed to help. Eventually, she was prescribed multiple medications to mitigate the diagnoses of attention-deficit/hyperactivity disorder (ADHD) and depression.

Throughout this journey, no one questioned Alison's relationship with her smartphone.

During our consultation, I couldn't help but notice her proximity to her smartphone. She held it tightly as though it were a lifeline, barely letting go, even during our conversation. She placed it on her lap while I examined her and only parted with it when I asked her to step on the scale.

> **Throughout this journey, no one questioned Alison's relationship with her smartphone.**

I felt compelled to gently approach the issue. I found that Alison was spending an average of 41 hours a week on her smartphone, primarily on YouTube and social media. She shrugged it off, justifying it as "quite normal for people her age." Although I didn't doubt her, I asked if she would be willing to show me what kind of content she typically watched. As she rapidly scrolled her feed for me, I saw what I had expected. Her screen was filled with "What I eat in a day" videos, body transformation clips, restrictive meal plans, and influencers promoting unrealistic beauty standards. Essentially, disordered eating under the guise of "fitness."

I gently suggested that her excessive screen time and consumption of toxic online content might be linked to a possible eating disorder.[15,16] Furious, Alison stormed out of the exam room, leaving her tearful mother behind.

In his book, *Self-Unfoldment*, Swami Chinmayananda describes two fundamental life choices: the path of the pleasant and the path of the challenge. We often know what is beneficial for us and what isn't, yet many times, we choose a path that is not beneficial to our well-being. At every single moment of our lives, we are confronted with the choice of one of the two paths. The path of the pleasant brings instant gratification, but it often leads to long-term regret and disappointment. On the other hand, the path of the challenge may involve discomfort and trials at the start, but it promises fulfillment and happiness in the long run.

The choices that lie ahead

As you explore strategies to break the trigger loop of wireless mobile devices (WMDs), you will frequently face this choice. I encourage you to pause the impulse of doing things the way *you have always done* or the way *everyone does* and find the courage to step out of cultural norms that are not uplifting you. Imagine the joy, peace, and happiness that lie on the other side. The path of the pleasant might lure you into spending more time on your WMD or giving your teenager a WMD. However, the path of the challenge will help you regain your time, focus, and well-being, and perhaps the audacity to say no to WMD and heavy social media use by your young child, leading to better long-term outcomes.

Once more, let's revisit the four steps of the trigger loop of WMDs:

Cue → Craving → Response → Reward

Here is a stepwise approach that can be used to break this cycle:

(Step-by-step video tutorial is available in the Resources section at calmthenoise.info)

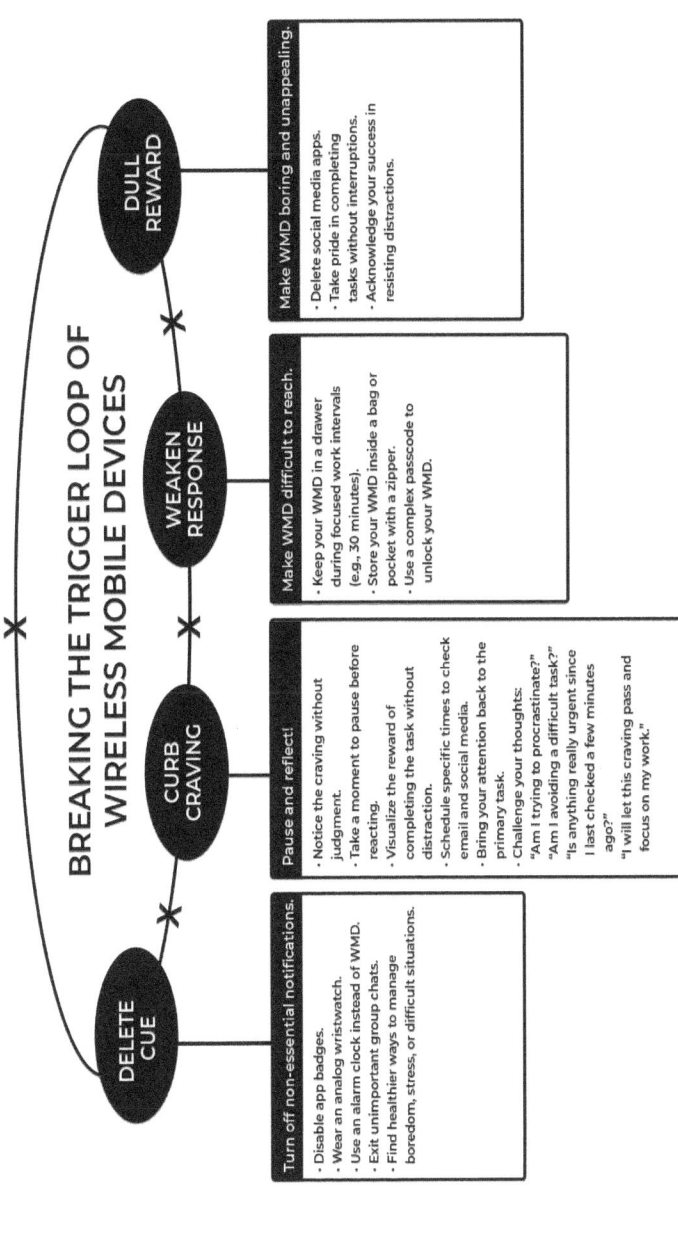

BREAKING THE TRIGGER LOOP OF WIRELESS MOBILE DEVICES

DELETE CUE

CURB CRAVING

WEAKEN RESPONSE

DULL REWARD

Turn off non-essential notifications.

- Disable app badges.
- Wear an analog wristwatch.
- Use an alarm clock instead of WMD.
- Exit unimportant group chats.
- Find healthier ways to manage boredom, stress, or difficult situations.

Pause and reflect!

- Notice the craving without judgment.
- Take a moment to pause before reacting.
- Visualize the reward of completing the task without distraction.
- Schedule specific times to check email and social media.
- Bring your attention back to the primary task.
- Challenge your thoughts: "Am I trying to procrastinate?" "Am I avoiding a difficult task?" "Is anything really urgent since I last checked a few minutes ago?" "I will let this craving pass and focus on my work."

Make WMD difficult to reach.

- Keep your WMD in a drawer during focused work intervals (e.g., 30 minutes).
- Store your WMD inside a bag or pocket with a zipper.
- Use a complex passcode to unlock your WMD.

Make WMD boring and unappealing.

- Delete social media apps.
- Take pride in completing tasks without interruptions.
- Acknowledge your success in resisting distractions.

Practical strategies to break the trigger loop by interrupting the cycle at four key steps: cue, craving, response, and reward. By reducing notifications, pausing before reacting, making your WMD harder to access, and finding satisfaction in focused work, you can regain control over your time and attention.

Step 1: Delete the *cues* that facilitate engagement with WMDs

- Turn off non-essential notifications.
  Notifications act as repetitive cues that trigger the loop. By silencing them, you reduce the number and frequency of external stimuli that prompt mindless engagement with your WMD.

- Disable badges.
  Red notification badges signal urgency and lure you into applications (apps) unnecessarily. Removing them prevents the cue of *something is waiting for you* and thus breaks the initial pull into the loop.

- Wear an analog wristwatch.
  Each glance at your WMD to check the time can spiral into unintended distractions. A wristwatch eliminates that cue entirely.

- Use an alarm clock.
  The simple act of setting an alarm on your WMD often leads to late-night doomscrolling. An alarm clock ensures that your WMD stays out of reach during these crucial wind-down times.

- Find alternative ways to handle boring or challenging situations.
  Boredom often drives WMD use. Alternative activities like reading, walking, stretching, or resting replace the need to rely on your WMD to escape monotony.

Step 2: Curb the dopamine-driven *craving* to check WMDs

- Be mindful of the irrational craving.
  Acknowledge the craving as a *momentary urge* rather than an *immediate need*. Awareness weakens the intensity of the craving.

- Ease into the craving without judgment.
  Rather than reacting impulsively and giving in to the cue, take a moment to recognize the craving, and create a pause between the cue and your response.

- Handle cravings differently.
  When you feel the urge to check your WMD, pause, stretch, blink, hydrate, and move around. Physical activity interrupts the habitual response to cravings and redirects energy toward productive behaviors.

- Bring mindfulness to the primary task.
  Fully immersing yourself in your current activity shifts focus from the WMD to the task at hand, reducing the power of cravings.

- Anticipate the positive reward from completing a task without distraction.

- Address the procrastination impulse directly.
  Use reflective questions and statements such as:
  "I know I am trying to avoid this task, but I will feel much better finishing it without distractions."

  "Am I trying to procrastinate?"

"Am I trying to avoid a tough situation?"

"I am sure nothing new has happened since I last checked a few minutes ago."

"I will let this craving pass and focus on work."

Step 3: Weaken the *response*

- Physically separate yourself from your WMD.
  Store your WMD in a drawer during work hours and avoid accessing it for 30-minute blocks. Over time, increase the duration of these uninterrupted blocks.

- Write down intrusive thoughts.
  Keep a notepad handy to jot down any distractions that come to mind during work. This prevents you from breaking focus while still acknowledging your thoughts.

- Turn off biometric unlocking (like Face ID or fingerprint) and use a complex passcode instead.
  Making your WMD less accessible introduces a layer of friction, reducing impulsive use.

Step 4: Dull the *reward*

- Remind yourself that your WMD is a tool, not a distraction.
  Reframing your perspective reduces the emotional reward tied to checking your WMD unnecessarily.

- Delete time-consuming apps.
  Removing social media and other time-consuming apps diminishes the instant gratification of scrolling. Access these platforms via a web browser when necessary.

- Keep only essential apps on the home screen.
  A minimalist home screen eliminates the visual cues that trigger the urge to open apps.

- Triage apps into folders.
  Move apps into folders so that they are not immediately visible, making it less likely that you will engage with them mindlessly.

It has been five months since Alison stormed out of my office, angry at the suggestion that her WMD overuse might be contributing to her eating disorder. Her mother, however, recognized the deeper issue and felt strongly about initiating digital wellness coaching for the family. Recently, I received a text message from her. Alison had refused to consider any form of digital wellness coaching. Instead, her ADHD and antidepressant medication doses had been increased.

I replied, with a heavy heart, "I am so sorry I wasn't able to help."

Sometimes, the path of the challenge is harder to walk, but it is always there, waiting for us to choose it when we are ready.

Your Actionable Recap

- The *pleasant* path may lead to more WMD use, but choosing the *challenging* path helps reclaim time, focus, and well-being.
- The four steps to breaking the trigger loop of WMDs are:
  - Delete the cues
  - Curb the craving
  - Weaken the response
  - Dull the reward

Yes, but ... What if ... How about?

- **Yes, but I will feel left out if I am not active on social media. That is the only way I talk to my friends.**
  The anxiety of feeling disconnected or being left out is completely valid, especially in a world where social media is the dominant form of interaction. It is challenging to go *countercultural*. But it's important to ask yourself: "Even with full access to social media, do I sometimes still feel left out?" Consider those group chats you were not included in or the events you saw on social media that you were not invited to. If you already feel some form of exclusion despite being on social media, perhaps trying the other side—in other words, reducing your reliance on it—might offer a different sense of connection and peace.

  In my work with digital wellness, I have met many parents who are building communities of like-minded families, where their kids grow up without heavy social media use. They are intentional about creating opportunities for offline socializing. Similarly, I have come across teens and young adults who deliberately stay off social media because they find that it doesn't serve them. Like finding online friends, making the effort to cultivate genuine, offline friendships can lead to deeper and more meaningful connections that do not rely on constant scrolling.

  By stepping back from social media, you may find yourself feeling less affected by the fear of missing out.

- **What if I need to access my WMD at work constantly for two-factor authentication?**
Yes, that's a valid concern, and it can prevent you from stowing your WMD away for 30-minute focus blocks. Two-factor authentication (2FA) is essential for security, and unfortunately, it requires frequent access to your WMD. However, the real issue arises when you find your screen bombarded with notifications while you are reaching for the code. By the time you finish scrolling through distractions, the 2FA code might have expired!

  This is where turning off non-essential notifications, disabling app badges, and removing time-draining apps can be game changers.

  Without the temptation of unread notifications and enticing red badges, your WMD becomes more of a tool rather than a distraction. By reducing these triggers, you are less likely to fall into a dopamine-driven loop when reaching for your verification code, allowing you to get back to work quickly and efficiently.

- **How about after hours? Can I spend some time doomscrolling in the evening?**
A little bit of indulgence here and there is fine! The key is to be mindful of how much time you are spending and whether other essential activities are being neglected, if any. For example, in a marriage, is one partner left doing most of the chores after a long workday while the other is taking an extended doomscrolling break on a WMD? Or does a student keep putting off assignments for *just a few more minutes* of scrolling, only to struggle to stop?

Does bedtime get pushed back because you are caught in the cycle of last-minute scrolling?

By being aware of these situations, you can inject a level of intentionality into your actions. Pausing to reflect on whether your scrolling is truly relaxation or just procrastination will help you shape a healthier relationship with your WMD.

Part 2
The Why

5
Why Are We Obsessed with Screens?

We are just beginning to understand how these digital environments are reshaping our emotional lives.

—**Jonathan Haidt**

I spotted Riley's name on my afternoon patient list. Riley, a 17-year-old young lady with type 1 diabetes mellitus, and her mother, drive one and a half hours each way to my clinic for her diabetes management. Now, before you think I have earned some coveted TOP DOCTOR title in their local magazine (spoiler: I haven't), let me tell you, it's simply because pediatric endocrinologists are a rare entity in the United States. The population-to-endocrinologist ratio within 20 miles for children is 39,492:1,[17] which is about as likely as finding a charger when your wireless mobile device (WMD) battery is at 1 percent.

As I examined Riley, her mother chimed in, "Dr. Gupta, there's something else we need your expert opinion on. It might not be hormone-related, but could you please look?" She pointed to a rash on Riley's lower back. After a quick inspection, I turned to Riley's mother and said, "Riley has a bedsore on her lower back. I am surprised because typically I see bedsores in individuals who have been immobilized for a prolonged period."

Riley's mother's face froze. Her eyes widened, her lips began to quiver, and tears streamed down her cheeks. She took a big gulp of air and said, "Would it help you to know, Dr. Gupta, that from the minute Riley gets home from school, she bolts to her room, lies on her bed, puts her virtual reality glasses on—which unfortunately I paid for—and disappears into the digital universe until bedtime, sometimes even sleeping in that world?" She continued, "As soon as I pick Riley up from school, I cannot get home fast enough. Riley cannot tolerate stopping for groceries on the way back. It seems as if a strange mania overtakes her, and all she can focus on is getting home and losing herself in the virtual world, and there dare not be any interruptions from the real world."

Riley's story is not unique. Across the world, countless children and adults are slipping into the digital abyss. This pattern isn't just about excessive use—it is the hallmark of behavior addiction. Behavior addiction is defined in a variety of ways by mental health professionals. One such definition is:

Repeated failure to resist an impulse, drive, or urge to perform an act that is rewarding to the person (at least in the short-term), despite longer-term harm, either to the individual or to others.[18]

The key feature of all definitions of behavior addiction is:

Unsuccessful attempts to control the behavior.

Or more simply put, the inability to control our impulses, despite knowing that it's probably not the best idea.

In the past, I used to go to bed with my social media feeds always at my service to whisk me into the mind-numbing world of short videos. At the time, my habit felt innocuous, and even a tad entertaining and relaxing. Forty-five minutes later, I would still be scrolling, my mind fully stimulated and buzzing with all the information (perhaps *noise*?), photos, reels, videos, posts, and ads I had exposed my eyes and soul to. The fall in my melatonin level (i.e., the sleep-inducing hormone) due to the blue light exposure was palpable.[19,20] Then there were those nights when after the kids were tucked in, we would settle down to watch *just one episode* of the latest binge-worthy series. Six episodes later ...

I began to question the science behind WMD addiction. It turns out that the behavior patterns in addictive WMD users are strikingly similar to those seen in substance abusers.[21] While this might seem like stretching things too far, the evidence deserves consideration.

According to a study in the *American Journal of Psychiatry*, behavioral addictions, including those related to digital devices, activate the same neural pathways as substance addictions, particularly involving the release of dopamine in the brain's reward circuits.[22] Our collective addiction to WMDs has been considered one of the greatest non-drug addictions of the 21st century. It is crucial to identify the brain changes that underlie the transition from casual or recreational WMD use to dependency, and eventually, addiction.

Understanding digital addiction requires us to look at how our brains respond to rewards and reinforcement. Uncontrollable WMD use has been linked to the *incentive sensitization theory of addiction*: Repeated exposure to potentially addictive stimuli (e.g., notifications) might result in persistent changes in the brain.[23-25] These brain changes mainly involve parts of the prefrontal cortex. This is a crucial area of the brain that regulates executive functions, such as task initiation, emotional regulation, sustained attention, impulse control, and organization.

The prefrontal cortex also controls our reactions to cues (e.g., the craving to check the WMD in response to a cue/notification).[26] I would like to think of the prefrontal cortex as the Chief Executive Officer of the brain. But throw a WMD into the mix, and suddenly, it's like putting a toddler in charge of a candy store.

Executive functions allow us to regulate our behavior and keep ourselves planned, goal-oriented, flexible, and effective. These control processes are reduced in WMD over-users or addicts. This may be related to their loss of control over their WMD use. They are unable to curb the craving to check it every few seconds or minutes. To make matters worse is the ease and normalization of WMD use in all social contexts, even during driving and team meetings—tasks that require our focused attention.

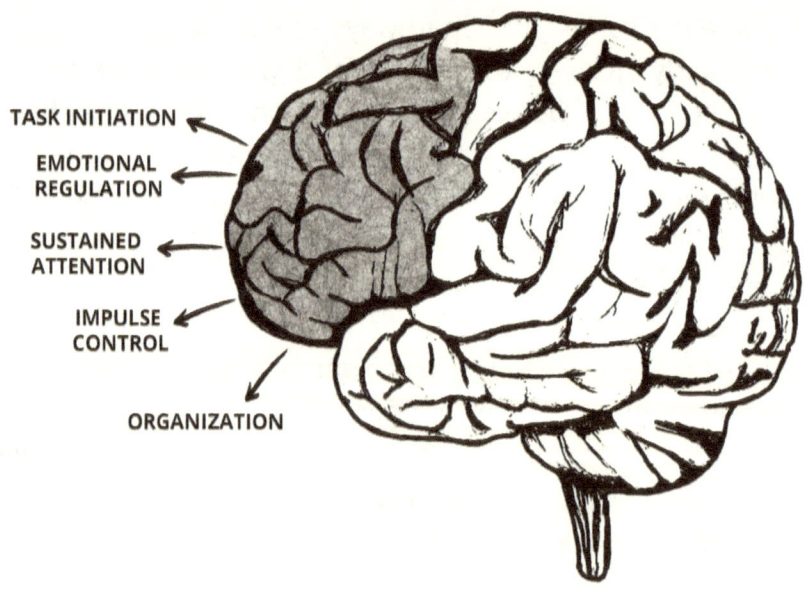

TASK INITIATION

EMOTIONAL REGULATION

SUSTAINED ATTENTION

IMPULSE CONTROL

ORGANIZATION

The prefrontal cortex

When confronted with complex real-life situations that require us to focus and resist internet-related cues/distractions (e.g., notifications on WMDs), we find it difficult to develop coping strategies. In a moment of conflict, it is all too easy to escape the situation, find the nearest bathroom, flush our sorrows (literally), and sometimes even post about it while we are at it.

> **Ingesting the noise of the online world is our ineffective attempt to drown out the noise within.**

Next, we find ourselves slipping down the never-ending trail of doomscrolling. Ingesting the noise of the online world is our ineffective attempt to drown out the noise within. Does the conflict go away, or did we temporarily manage to numb ourselves and procrastinate dealing with the negative situation?

While engaged with a WMD, the user receives positive reinforcement in terms of dysfunctional coping with daily life problems. The reinforcement/reward that is experienced when using WMDs then strengthens expectations for the next cue. Users may ignore healthier ways to cope with negative moods, boredom, emotions, stress, anxiety, or conflicts. Through a WMD, the internet and the exciting virtual world are *always there* to help us escape the feelings of real-life emotional or social loneliness.

The pattern of turning to WMDs for comfort not only reinforces the habit but also displaces essential activities. I call this the *Escape-Displace* theory, where WMDs facilitate an easy escape from real-life stress. In our unintentional pursuit of escape from these tough situations, we *displace* and procrastinate seemingly mundane tasks—sleeping, exercising, cooking healthy meals, meditating, spending screen-free quality time with children, being efficient at work and school, and so on. The excessive amount of leisurely time spent on WMDs displaces the time that could or should have been spent on these essential activities. The perceived boredom of these tasks cannot compete with the dopamine-driven pleasures of the online world.

The combination of positive reinforcement from the content found on WMDs and the thrill of its novel pleasures results in ignoring the need to cope with negative situations in the real world. This also drives the procrastination of common school or office-related tasks, just like in my own story presented at the beginning of this book. When we are exposed to such strong reinforcement from the content found on our WMDs, the cure of *disconnecting* from them needs to be equally resilient and mindful.

The pull of the WMDs isn't just about the device. It's about the carefully designed experiences that keep us coming back. Before we move forward, let's remind ourselves of the fundamental truth:

The device (WMD) is just the medium. It is merely a tool.
The addiction is not to the device.
The addiction is to the content.
The addiction is to distraction.
The addiction is to the need to avoid boredom.
The addiction is to the feeling of being informed.

For some, like my patient Riley, recognizing this reality is the initial step in a long and difficult journey. The discovery of the bedsore was just the beginning of an uphill battle for Riley. It later turned out

Riley is slowly learning to *ungrip* WMDs and *grip* life.

that her bedsore was in fact six inches deep underneath her skin and had to be surgically resected. Because Riley has type 1 diabetes mellitus, her post-surgical healing took longer than usual. The next time I met Riley, I saw tears again—but this time, they were tears of joy, and they were Riley's, not her mother's. Through our work together, Riley is slowly learning to *ungrip* WMDs and *grip* life. Riley is learning to detox so that she can stay connected while continuing to remain healthy.

DELETE THE CUES

Instead of

Change the environment that triggers unhealthy habits

CURB THE CRAVING

Instead of

Counter the craving with logic

WEAKEN THE RESPONSE

Instead of

Physically separate yourself

DULL THE REWARD

Instead of

Find joy in real life connections

Your Actionable Recap

- Behavior addiction is characterized by an unsuccessful attempt to control behavior.
- Behavior patterns in addictive WMD users are similar to those observed among substance abusers.
- Repeated exposure to notifications can result in persistent changes in the brain.
- The prefrontal cortex controls reactions to cues; WMD overuse disrupts its normal functioning.
- Coping strategies must be built and strengthened in the real world.
- While we escape from boredom and anxiety, we also displace essential activities of daily living.

Yes, but ... What if ... How about?

- **Yes, but what is the harm in scrolling through social media before bed? It really helps me sleep better!**
  While it might feel relaxing at the moment, scrolling through social media or any other content on your WMD before bed disrupts your sleep cycle. The blue light from screens suppresses melatonin production, making it harder for you to fall asleep and reducing the quality of your sleep.

- **What if I am still able to sleep for eight hours after scrolling through social media or binge-watching Netflix?**
  Even if you manage to get eight hours of sleep, the quality of that sleep might be compromised. The overstimulation from screen use before bed can prevent you from reaching the deeper stages of sleep that are essential for rest and recovery.

- **How about adults whose brains have completely formed already? I am sure this phenomenon impacts growing children only.**
  While it's true that children are more vulnerable to the impact of WMD overuse because their brains are still developing, adults are not immune. The prefrontal cortex, which is responsible for decision-making, impulse control, and managing emotions, remains sensitive to the overstimulation caused by constant screen use.

  Even in fully developed brains, excessive WMD use can impair these functions, leading to difficulties in concentration, and increased impulsivity. Over time, this can contribute to an increased risk of mental health issues, such as anxiety and depression. So, while the impact might be more pronounced in children, adults are far from exempt from the negative effects of WMD overuse.

6
Why Are Smart Devices So Addictive?

Our phones steal our attention and keep us coming back for more, often at the expense of our real lives.
—**Catherine Price**

I was 28 weeks pregnant when the world started closing down in response to the COVID-19 pandemic. As I wrapped up my workday that Friday evening, a looming sense of uncertainty lingered—I might not return to work on Monday. I also was worried about COVID-19's impact on pregnant women and the babies they carried.

Over that weekend, COVID-19 swept through the globe like wildfire, leaving us all scrambling for safety goggles, masks, hand sanitizers, and toilet paper. Healthcare professionals across the nation switched to telemedicine, grappling with the uncertainties of the unknown virus. Suddenly, my quest for information about COVID-19 went into overdrive. Why? Well, it turns out that there is something about being *informed* that triggers an ancient part of our brains—the parts that developed at a time when knowing where the nearest danger lurked could make the difference between eating dinner and becoming dinner.

In their highly acclaimed book, *The Distracted Mind*, neuro-scientist Adam Gazzaley and psychologist Larry D. Rosen describe the responses of the ancient brain confronted by a high-tech world.[27] They suggest that our primal survival instincts now manifest as a craving for information. It is as if our brains are programmed to seek out information—only instead of predators, we are now haunted by news updates, weather forecasts, stocks, politics, sports, business, gossip, and the latest TikTok trends.

Each juicy *byte* of information sends a wave of relief washing over us—relief at soothing the craving for more information. But just as quickly as the relief sets in, so does the anticipation: What is next on the agenda? We turn quickly to the next nearest source of information through our wireless mobile devices (WMDs): social media, emails, news, weather, and so on.

Nearly three decades ago, two psychologists, Terry Robinson and Kent Berridge, explored the impact of illicit drugs on human psychology.[11] As discussed in Chapter 5, they developed the *incentive sensitization theory of addiction*, which suggested that repeated exposure to addictive stimuli (such as alcohol and drugs) could create permanent changes in brain cells. They noted that these stimuli might have an impact on brain circuits that normally regulate executive functions. Interestingly, although their theories focused on generalized addiction (i.e., drugs), their concepts seem to fit well with WMD addiction.

Changes in the functioning of dopamine pathways in the brain might explain our loss of control over WMD use. We talked about the prefrontal cortex in Chapter 5. There are additional regions of the brain linked to motivation and behavior: the basal ganglia and the nucleus accumbens,[23,24] which are regions of the brain that send dopamine signals to the prefrontal cortex, thereby completing the *motivation* loop and influencing impulse control and emotional regulation. Excessive exposure to digital stimuli may disrupt these brain circuits, impairing our ability to resist the urge to check our devices.

In the late 1890s, Ivan Pavlov introduced a theory that revolutionized our understanding of learned behavior.[28] Born in 1849 in Russia, Pavlov performed a groundbreaking experiment involving dogs that enhanced our understanding of how new habits develop through repeated associations between independent stimuli. Pavlov observed that dogs naturally salivated when presented with food; this is an example of an unconditioned stimulus. However, by repeating a neutral stimulus, such as a bell that sounded as the food was presented, the dogs eventually began to associate the bell with the arrival of food. As a result, the dogs started salivating at the sound of the bell alone, even in the absence of the food.

WMD overuse can be viewed as analogous to the example of Pavlov's dog. In humans, social interaction results in dopamine release, while a neutral stimulus (e.g., a communication device) might not have this effect. During conditioning, the brain associates WMD notifications with social interactions. After conditioning, WMD notifications result in dopamine release in anticipation of the human connection. Ultimately, the visual cue provided by the WMD alone results in dopamine release even in the absence of any notifications (e.g., checking the device for no reason). In this way, the human brain can become conditioned in a Pavlovian manner to release dopamine in response to reward-related cues. The appearance of the cue, or simply the anticipation of its appearance, produces pulses of high dopamine release, brain activation, and motivations that last for a few seconds or minutes.

Conditioning the human brain like Pavlov's dog

Certain brain states such as stress and boredom amplify the intensity of the urge to check the WMD. For example, the stress of the unknown COVID-19 virus and the boredom of remote working without real human connection made me constantly reach for my WMD, hoping for that next hit of dopamine-induced euphoria.

Although the dopamine-induced brain activation lasts for only a few seconds, the intensity of these urges is so strong that it is nearly impossible for WMD users to stop at just checking a message. The amplified urge snowballs from the simple act of picking up the WMD and checking just one message to checking other notifications, flitting from one application to another, browsing multiple social media platforms, and eventually losing track

> **WMDs have become an extension of us; a virtual fifth limb.**

of time. Not only do we waste precious time, but we also get distracted and lose focus, and efficiency.

WMDs have become an extension of us; a virtual fifth limb. They remain at the bedside, under the pillow, or in a pocket and are used in the restroom, while driving, at work, during meals, in meetings, after hours, in restaurants, at social gatherings, at sleepovers, on playgrounds, on weekends, and during vacations. It is a vicious cycle of anticipation, distraction, and reward/disappointment.

The constant state of alertness takes a toll on our mental well-being, leading to heightened anxiety and a loss of perspective on reality. The unpredictability of the WMD content (when it might show up and what it might look like) keeps us guessing and on tenterhooks, much like slot machines do. The mind stays vigilant and releases dopamine spikes in short bursts, in anticipation of what might come next.

On the other end of the spectrum, the absence of a notification, a like, or a positive comment on social media deflates the amplified sense of anticipation, leading to dopamine dip. Irrational feelings of sadness, loneliness, or isolation, or of feeling outcast, unwanted, uncared for, or even panicky about creating irrelevant content, take over. The distinction between the *real* and *the reel* (literally) is extinguished.

In adolescents, the phenomenon of (un-)acceptance on social media has clearly led to a significant increase in the incidence of anxiety, depression, and suicides over the past decade. A study published in *JAMA Pediatrics* found that adolescents who spent more than three hours per day on social media were significantly more likely to report high levels of internalizing behaviors, including symptoms of anxiety and depression.[29] Similarly, the U.S. Centers for Disease Control and Prevention reported a 56 percent increase in suicide rates among people aged 10–24 years between 2007 and 2015, a period that coincides with the rise of social media.[30] These findings suggest a disturbing correlation between prolonged social media use and the deterioration of mental health in young people.

It would be naïve for us as adults to think that we are immune to the impact of feelings that emerge in response to images, reels, and all the other chaos and noise we expose ourselves to in the online world. In fact, there is a significant correlation between social media use and increased levels of anxiety in adults. A study published in *Computers in Human Behavior* found that adults who used social media for more than two hours a day were more likely to experience anxiety symptoms compared to those who used it less frequently.[31]

Clearly, data suggests that even in fully developed brains, excessive social media use can contribute to heightened anxiety and overall mental distress. Another study in *The Journal of Social and Clinical Psychology* revealed that reducing social media use to 30 minutes a day resulted in significant reductions in anxiety, depression, loneliness, and FOMO.[32]

In those quiet moments, away from the noisy screens, I found a sense of calm that no number of online updates could ever provide.

As for me, well, let's just say I soaked up all COVID-19-related information until I could take no more. If my relationship with my WMD was different at the time, perhaps a less stressful story would have unfolded—maybe one with fewer notifications and more naps. Eventually, I chose to disconnect from the relentless flood of information. I found myself more grounded, more present, and more connected to the loved ones in my COVID-19 bubble.

The world may have been chaotic, and the uncertainty overwhelming, but stepping back from the digital chaos allowed me to focus on what truly mattered. In those quiet moments, away from the noisy screens, I found a sense of calm that no number of online updates could ever provide. And now, as I look into my son's bright, curious eyes, I am reminded that sometimes, the best way to stay connected is simply to unplug.

Your Actionable Recap

- The addiction is not to the device itself but to the feeling of being informed and the constant need for distraction.
- Dopamine, the anticipation hormone, is released in response to notifications and the glow of the screen, and drives our compulsion to check our devices.
- Excessive exposure to digital stimuli can disrupt impulse control and emotional regulation, leading to addictive behaviors.
- Stress and boredom amplify the urge to check the WMDs and can turn a quick glance into a time-consuming habit.
- The absence of notifications or social media engagement can lead to irrational feelings of sadness, loneliness, and inadequacy.
- The issues of social media and WMD overuse affect not only adolescents but adults as well, contributing to anxiety and mental health challenges across all ages.

Yes, but ... What if ... How about?

- **Yes, but isn't staying informed during times of crisis, like a pandemic, more important than ever?**
  Staying informed is indeed necessary, especially during times of crisis, but there is a fine line between being informed and being overinformed or misinformed. Constantly consuming digital information can increase anxiety and lead to burnout. It is crucial to set boundaries, consume information mindfully, and take breaks to stay grounded and protect your mental health.

Additionally, not all information available online is accurate; some of it can create unnecessary concern and divisiveness. The algorithms behind digital platforms often feed users information based on their existing preferences, creating a *filter bubble* where users see what they want to see rather than what they need to see or what is true. This can distort reality and reinforce biases, making it even more important to approach digital information with caution.

- **What if I feel anxious when I am not constantly checking my phone for updates?**
  Feeling anxious when you are not checking your phone might be a sign that your brain has become dependent on the dopamine hits resulting from constant updates. This is a common response, but it can be managed. Gradually reducing screen time and engaging in practical strategies reviewed in *Calm the Noise* can help you regain control and reduce anxiety.

- **How about addiction to food? Does that co-exist with addiction to screens?**
  Yes, food addiction can often coexist with addiction to screens. Both types of addiction are driven by similar brain mechanisms, particularly the dopamine pathways that respond to rewards. When we use screens, especially for activities like social media or gaming, our brains release dopamine, which creates a feeling of pleasure and reinforces the behavior. The same process occurs with food, especially with highly palatable foods rich in sugar, fat, and salt.

When screen time and eating overlap—for instance, snacking while watching TV or scrolling through your phone—it creates a reinforcing cycle where the brain seeks out both digital and food-related rewards simultaneously. Unhealthy habits form and the challenges of managing screen time and eating behaviors are exacerbated.

Part 3
The Who

7
Who Is at the Greatest Risk for Developing Digital Addiction?

The chains of habit are too weak to be felt
until they are too strong to be broken.
—**Samuel Johnson**

I first met Victor and his parents in my office for a digital wellness coaching session. Victor was teetering on the brink of suspension from college due to chronically delinquent assignments and a notable absence from classes. His parents were at their wits' end. Victor described his daily routine: *"I play video games with my old school friends until 4 a.m., go to bed, wake up around noon, eat, attend a couple of classes if I feel like it, come back, check my phone here and there, do a few other things, chat with friends, eat dinner, and resume playing video games."*

As I got to know Victor and his family better, he allowed me to peek into the screen time data on his wireless mobile device (WMD) (in this case, his smartphone). Video games do not yet come with screen time monitoring data! His smartphone screen time averaged about five to six hours per day with Netflix, Discord, and Reddit being the top contenders. Once I had managed to wrap my head around Victor's monumental daily screen time (five to six hours on his smartphone, plus five to six hours of video gaming), we began our work.

Victor's story was more complex than just the hours spent in front of a screen. When he was 16, he discovered that his father, a successful businessman, had a penchant for pornography. His father's own relationship with WMDs and video gaming bordered on addiction. Victor's father had had a challenging childhood and was resistant to seeking professional help to address his mental health. Victor's mom, on the other hand, was doing her best to hold the family together.

Years passed. Victor somehow made it through school and got into a local community college. A couple of years later, his mother filed for divorce. Victor's world fell apart. Growing up in a dysfunctional family environment and immersed in his digital pursuits, he had never had the chance to develop effective coping strategies. He felt disconnected, hurt, helpless, and lonely. While he had used video games and WMDs during his school years, he now leaned on these digital crutches even more. The hedonic pleasures from screens and the violent nature of the video games he played helped to numb his pain. As he casually remarked one day, "At least, I'm not doing drugs."

Victor's experience highlights how multiple factors can contribute to digital addiction. But what makes some individuals more vulnerable than others? It is equally important to emphasize that not all WMD users transition from casual use to dependency and addiction. Some people manage to use WMDs judiciously to their advantage, whether to advance their business, stay updated on global developments, or keep in touch with distant family members. So, why do others struggle to control their WMD use?

There are several possible explanations for why some individuals are more vulnerable to WMD addiction than others.[33,34]

- **Genetic factors**
  Genetics plays a strong role in addiction vulnerability, including behavioral addictions like WMD overuse.
- **Personality traits**
  Certain dysfunctional personality traits can foster WMD addiction.[35] Traits like poor self-discipline, low cooperativeness, social anxiety, shyness, and a tendency toward procrastination are particularly influential.[36] These traits may lead individuals to use WMDs as a coping mechanism, seeking solace in digital interactions rather than facing real-world challenges.
- **Social factors**
  Social factors, including a lack of real-life social support, feelings of social isolation, loneliness, and depression, significantly nurture WMD addiction.[37,38] People who feel disconnected from those around them may turn to their WMDs for a sense of connection, even if the relationships they form online are superficial.
- **Gender differences**
  Gender can also influence susceptibility to WMD addiction.[39] Research suggests that men may be more prone to video game addiction, while women are more likely to become addicted to social media.[40] These gender differences are partially due to varying motivations for screen use: Men often seek competition and a sense of achievement, whereas women may seek social connection and emotional support through their WMDs.
- **Boredom and life stressors**
  A tendency toward boredom and the presence of significant life stressors can increase the risk of developing unhealthy WMD habits.[41] People who struggle with boredom or have experienced major stressors, such as family conflict, academic pressure, or trauma, may be more likely to use WMDs as an escape.

A combination of these factors may further increase the risk of developing unhealthy WMD use.

Maladaptive cognition about the world, coupled with excessive internet use via WMDs and a tendency to seek an escape from the real world, may intensify the transition toward WMD addiction in vulnerable individuals. Prolonged, high-dose WMD use can lead to neural dopaminergic hyper-reactivity, similar to drug addiction.

Individual features that increase the risk of transition to WMD overuse

Genetics
Personality traits
• Low self-esteem • Low self-control • Low conscientiousness • Low agreeableness • Social anxiety • Shyness • Procrastination tendencies • Maladaptive cognition about the world • Difficulty with conflict • Impulsivity and sensation seeking (thrill and adventure seeking) • Intolerance of pain and sadness • Lack of inhibition • Sensitivity to boredom
Social factors
• Lack of social support in real life • Feelings of social isolation • Loneliness
Other factors
• Age at first cell phone < 13 years • Tendency towards depressive or dysphoric states • Major stressors in life before WMD use • Excessive internet use via WMD
*A combination of these factors increases the risk further

Understanding these risk factors is important, especially when deciding when to introduce children to WMDs. This leads to one of the most thought-provoking and highly debated questions in the modern parenting world:

What is the right age to introduce WMDs to a child?

I wish the answer was as simple as saying *wait until 8, 14, 18 years, or never*! However, the reality is far more complex, as each child's individual personality, environment, and development must be considered.

The introduction of WMDs to children is not a one-size-fits-all scenario. I encourage families to assess their child's personality at baseline before making decisions about WMD use. If a child exhibits several of the traits described above, the risk of developing WMD addiction increases significantly. Moreover, these underlying personality traits might worsen after introducing the WMD, especially if the screen time is not carefully managed.

Data from multiple countries suggest that the highest screen time is seen in adolescents, around the age of 14.[42] This is a critical period associated with developmental changes, including a temporary decline in self-control. Adolescents are in a phase where they are developing their identities, seeking social acceptance, and exploring independence.

The prefrontal cortex, the region of the brain responsible for executive functions that include decision-making, impulse control, and emotional regulation, does not fully mature until the mid-20s. The underdevelopment of the prefrontal cortex means that adolescents are particularly vulnerable to the temptations of WMDs, as they may lack the cognitive maturity to regulate their use effectively.[43] Expecting adolescents to exercise full self-control over their WMD use is, therefore, somewhat unrealistic.

Repeated exposure to potentially addictive stimuli, such as notifications from WMDs, can cause permanent changes in the prefrontal cortex, further complicating the development of self-regulation. Unsurprisingly, higher levels of WMD addiction are found in those who receive their first smartphone before the age of 13.[44] The early exposure often correlates with greater screen time during the adolescent years, leading to a cycle where increased screen time exacerbates the very traits that make WMD addiction more likely.

In addition to cognitive and behavioral concerns, early and excessive WMD use can have other consequences, such as disrupted sleep patterns, increased risk of mental health issues like anxiety and depression, and diminished face-to-face social interactions. Given these risks, it is essential for parents and guardians to not only consider the age at which they introduce WMDs but also to remain vigilant about the content their children consume and the amount of time they spend on these devices.

As exposure to WMDs increases, a troubling phenomenon emerges—tolerance. Is it possible to develop a tolerance to the pleasures derived from WMD use and ultimately seek more stimulation than the WMDs can provide? Yes! Just like with other addictive behaviors, the more we use, the more stimulation we need to feel satisfied.

Researchers have found that increased screen time, especially exposure to harmful content, could trigger substance use, alcohol use, cigarette smoking, violence, and risky sexual behavior.[45] There seems to be a dose-response relationship between the hours of screen time and these adverse effects. However, it would be naïve to imagine that increased screen time alone is enough to trigger these behaviors. The basis for this association is likely multifactorial.

Repeated and prolonged exposure to video games in young adults like Victor may cause desensitization to the pleasures of the game.[45] Then, they require higher levels of stimulation to get the same *kick* out of it. They might then turn to substances and pornography to compensate for the reduced experience of pleasure. This phenomenon could manifest as an absence of motivation to pursue fulfilling tasks (e.g., a hobby) or essential responsibilities (e.g., college assignments).

A habitual WMD user might not find the usual content stimulating enough, which prompts the content developers to make their material more attention-grabbing and addictive. Content developers are well-versed in human psychology. In fact, they are often incentivized to apply the principles of behavior addiction to create content that is novel, exciting, adventurous, malicious, violent, and even sexual. The goal is to keep the WMD user *coming back for more*, maximizing the time spent on these devices and platforms.[46,47]

With companies designing digital platforms to maximize engagement, young people like Victor often become collateral damage in the attention economy. After several months of weekly coaching sessions which included education, exercises, hands-on activities, journaling, collaboration with psychologists, hope, despair, smiles, and tears, Victor felt what he described as a breath of fresh air. While he is not completely out of the woods yet, he has shown the courage and willingness to embark upon his digital wellness journey.

He aims to reconnect with his old school friends in a new way and learn skills to ensure that he stays connected with himself.

Victor felt what he described as a breath of fresh air.

Your Actionable Recap

- Genetics, personality traits, and social factors increase vulnerability to WMD addiction.
- Adolescents are at a higher risk due to underdeveloped self-control and executive functions.
- Assess your child's personality at baseline before making decisions about WMD use.
- Early exposure to WMDs, especially before age 13, is linked to higher levels of addiction.
- Tolerance to screen pleasures can lead to seeking more intense or harmful content.

Yes, but ... What if ... How about?

- **Yes, but isn't it normal for teenagers to spend a lot of time on their WMDs?**
  While it is *common* for teenagers to spend a lot of time on their WMDs, this does not make it *normal* or healthy. Addiction often starts with the normalization of certain behaviors, and unfortunately, we have come to accept excessive screen time as a typical part of adolescence. For this reason, parents find it difficult to recognize and address the behavior as problematic.

  My adolescent clients frequently tell me that their peers spend even more time online than they do, so they assume it must be okay. The real issue isn't just the amount of time spent on their phones; it is what opportunities for growth, learning, and real-life interactions are being missed during that time. What could have happened during that time instead?

- **What if my child seems happy, well-adjusted, and gets all As in school despite spending hours on their WMDs?**

  Even if your child seems happy and is doing well now, prolonged and excessive screen time can have cumulative effects that may not be apparent immediately. Over time, it can contribute to issues like reduced motivation, difficulty in social interactions, and even mental health challenges. Progressive impact on the developing brain can also influence your child's ability to learn, memorize, recall, and retain. Ultimately, tolerance to screen pleasures can lead to seeking more intense or harmful content.

- **How about the impact on mental health if my child is the only one without a WMD (smartphone) among their friends?**

  It is understandable to worry about your child feeling left out or isolated if they are the only one without a WMD. Social belonging is crucial during adolescence, and being different from their peers can be challenging. However, it is also important to weigh this against the lifelong mental health risks associated with early WMD use.

  Studies have now shown beyond a doubt that excessive screen time leads to increased anxiety, depression, and sleep disturbances. If your child is struggling with being the only one without a WMD, open communication is key. Discuss their feelings openly and find ways to support their social connections outside of digital interactions. You might need to make extra efforts to build a community of like-minded parents who are comfortable raising their children without WMDs. Getting buy-in from your school leadership for this initiative can also be incredibly helpful in creating a supportive environment.

8
Who Has the Strongest Bond with Their Devices?

It's not the technology itself that's the problem.
It's our relationship with it that needs to be examined.
—**Sherry Turkle**

Brenda is a retired schoolteacher and mother of two teenage daughters. A few years ago, she attended one of our workshops, *ReConnect*. Brenda brought her daughters along, noting that "They are going to learn the harms of being on their phone all the time!" The workshop attendees ranged from 8 to 65 years of age. I wasn't surprised by Brenda's goal as it echoed the sentiments of many parents in the room: teaching their kids a thing or two about their phones.

As the workshop progressed, I invited all attendees to take a 14-question survey: The Wireless Mobile Device (WMD) Balance Scale. As Brenda answered the questions on the survey, her face grew increasingly worried and deflated. I approached her and asked what the matter was. She was bewildered and said, "I scored higher on this survey than my daughters. I cannot believe it. OH MY GOSH! This is about me too!"

This realization—that our own relationships with WMDs might be more entangled than we think they are—is a wake-up call for many. We often focus on our children's screen time, believing that we, as adults, have everything under control. But the truth is, our own behaviors often mirror the very habits we want our children to avoid.

Here is a version of the WMD Balance Scale that Brenda took. I invite you to take the survey and answer each question with a Yes or No. The purpose of the survey is not to diagnose anyone with WMD addiction. This survey is simply meant to be used as a tool to gain insight into our relationship with our WMDs.

Before diving into the WMD Balance Scale, it is important to understand what is really at stake when we talk about our relationship with our devices. The impact of WMDs isn't just about screen time; it's about what we are losing in the process. Four key commodities—time, attention, sleep, and joy—are often sacrificed in the inferno of constant connectivity.

> **The impact of WMDs isn't just about screen time; it's about what we are losing in the process.**

As you go through the WMD Balance Scale, keep these four commodities in mind. The questions are designed to help you reflect on how your relationship with your WMD might be impacting these crucial areas of your life.

WMDs include smartphones, smartwatches, tablets, iPads, virtual reality eyewear, laptops, and all other screens including television, and video game systems.

The WMD Balance Scale

Purpose: Behavior assessment and learning scale for an undistracted, enjoyable life

QUESTION	YES	NO
TIME		
1. Do you find yourself mindlessly checking your WMD many times a day, even when you know there is likely nothing new or important to see?		
2. Do you seem to lose track of time when on your WMD?		
3. Do you regularly procrastinate important activities (work, assignments, exercise, sleep) due to your WMD use?		
4. Have your parents, partner, or friends complained about your WMD overuse (e.g., spending too much time in the toilet, on streaming channels, video gaming, or online shopping, etc.)?		
5. When your WMDs ring, beep, or glow, do you feel an intense urge to check for texts, posts, emails, updates, etc.?		
6. Do you wish you could be a little less involved with your WMD?		
ATTENTION		
7. Do you text, email, browse, or post while driving, working, or doing other similar activities that require your focused attention and concentration?		
8. Do you have your WMDs in mind even when you are not using them?		
SLEEP		
9. Do you sleep with your WMD near you (under the bed, near the bed, under your pillow, or on the bedside table) regularly?		
10. Do you spend time on your WMD right before you fall asleep?		
JOY		
11. Do you feel reluctant to be without your WMD, even for a short time?		
12. Do you feel bored when doing other stuff without your WMD?		
13. Does your WMD or social media use make you feel lonely?		
14. How often do you message/email people via your WMD when the people you are messaging/emailing are in the same room?		

Interpretation:

Now, count the number of Yes answers and tally them up. Here are possible interpretations of your score:

0–3 Yes answers: Your relationship with your WMD seems balanced. You are likely using it as a tool without letting it dominate your life.

4–7 Yes answers: Your WMD use is starting to take up more of your time and attention than might be healthy. It may be time to reassess and set some boundaries.

8–10 Yes answers: You may have developed a problematic or compulsive WMD use pattern. It might be worth exploring ways to reduce your dependency and regain control.

11–14 Yes answers: Your relationship with your WMD is deeply co-dependent and bordering on addiction. You might consider therapy to address the underlying issues that might be driving this behavior.

Your score might elicit laughter, surprise, grief, fear, anger, cynicism, acceptance, or disbelief. All these feelings are valid and welcome. My hope is that your score on the WMD Balance Scale was either a wake-up call or a reinforcement of what you already knew about your relationship with your WMDs.

Your score may have been eye-opening, but you are not alone. Around the world, researchers have developed different scales to assess WMD addiction, including in Korea, Taiwan, Spain, Brazil, France, Saudi Arabia, India, China, Iran, and Tibet.[10,48–56] The universal and cross-cultural nature of WMD addiction is undeniable and alarming.[57,58]

Despite differences in languages and cultures, common behavioral themes have emerged from the WMD addiction scales:

- Preoccupation with the WMD
- Using the WMD to escape or relieve a negative mood
- Spending more time on the WMD than initially intended
- Positive anticipation of *what is next*?
- Inability to focus on other activities
- Continued excessive use despite knowledge of the negative consequences
- Developing withdrawal symptoms such as irritability and anxiety when away from the device
- Unsuccessful attempts to cut down use
- Jeopardizing or losing a significant relationship
- Performing below expectations at one's job or in school

With the rise of WMD use, new disorders of the 21st century have emerged and are being recognized as:

- **Nomophobia (NO MObile PHone PhoBIA):** Fear of lack of access to a WMD[59,60]
- **Textaphrenia:** The false sensation of having received a text message, leading to constantly checking the WMD
- **Ringxiety:** The false sensation of having received a call, leading to constantly checking the WMD
- **Textiety:** Anxiety when receiving a text and feeling that one needs to respond immediately
- **Phubbing:** Focusing on the phone and unrelated calls or text messages while ignoring the persons who are present

Brenda's surprise at her WMD Balance Scale score compelled me to investigate the question of who got rewired first—was it adults or children? I found the answer to be both complex and revealing. Before children ever laid their hands on WMDs, adults had already normalized and passionately encouraged an all-encompassing digital culture. Many parents, like Brenda and me, believed that we were simply managing our work online while assuming that children were the ones at risk of screen addiction. However, science and experience tell a different story.

The behaviors we see in children—constant proximity to their WMDs, anxiety and the need to check them frequently, the inability to disconnect, anger when forced to disconnect, and emotional dependence on screens—are precisely the behaviors modeled by the adults in their lives.

Children are naturally keen observers. They will imitate what you do. When they see you scrolling through your WMD at the dinner table, reaching for your WMD while talking to your partner, quickly checking a text while driving, or vanishing into the bathroom with your WMD, they internalize these behaviors as normal.

Who, then, is the architect of a child's screen habits? The answer is simple: adults.

This realization is not meant to blame parents; rather, it highlights a shared responsibility. Adults who embraced technology as a tool but quickly allowed it to overtake their lives have inadvertently passed on this dependency to the next generation. The cycle will only break when we as adults acknowledge that digital wellness begins with us. By reclaiming our attention and redefining our relationships with WMDs, we not only

The cycle will only break when we as adults acknowledge that digital wellness begins with us.

improve our own lives but also set a powerful example for the young, impressionable minds that are watching us.

The day after the workshop, Brenda went hiking in the woods. She sent us a voice message:

"I must tell you. I just went on a hike. I put my phone in my backpack, and I didn't look at it the entire hour and fifteen minutes. And I am telling you, I am learning something. My heart has a much better memory than my damn smartphone does. I soaked up every step, crunch of the leaves, all the bird songs, everything. My family and I are on a mission now, and we are going to be in the moment!"

Your Actionable Recap

- Our own relationships with WMDs are often more entangled than we realize and may have a subtle impact on our physical, mental, and emotional well-being.
- WMD addiction scales have been developed globally, highlighting the universal nature of this concern.
- Common symptoms of WMD addiction include preoccupation, using devices to escape negative emotions, and developing withdrawal symptoms when away from the device.
- The cycle of digital addiction will only break when we, as adults, acknowledge that digital wellness begins with us.
- Every time we reach for our WMDs in the presence of our loved ones, we are sending them a message that something else is more valuable to us than they are.

Yes, but ... What if ... How about?

- **Yes, but how can I reduce my WMD use without feeling disconnected or anxious?**
  Start small by setting specific times during the day when you intentionally put your WMD away. Separate yourself physically from your WMD for at least 20–30 minutes each day. This intentional separation helps reduce dependency and anxiety over time. Replace this time with activities that genuinely engage you, for example, painting, gardening, singing, reading, cooking, writing, or spending time with loved ones. Gradually, you will find that the anxiety decreases as you reconnect with the real world and find more joy in it.

- **What if I rely on my WMD for work and social connections?**

  WMDs are essential tools for work and staying connected. The key is balance. Set boundaries for work-related use, such as not checking emails after a certain time, limiting the number of work-related apps on your WMD, and turning off notifications after hours (see Chapter 13). Building a work ethic where non-urgent communications can wait until the next business day and reducing reliance on texting for work can also help. Consider facilitating quick team meetings where all queries can be addressed in one concentrated period.

  If your professional or academic responsibilities demand extensive screen time, consider integrating regular breaks into your routine. Follow the 20-20-20 rule: After each 20-minute interval, look at something 20 feet away for 20 seconds to reduce eye strain.

- **How about using my WMD for positive habits, like mindfulness apps or learning tools?**

  Using your WMD for positive habits is a great way to harness its power without falling into unhealthy patterns. Just be mindful of not getting sucked into other distracting apps. Set limits on how long you use the device for these purposes to ensure it remains a tool for good rather than a source of stress and distraction.

Part 4
The How

9
How Does Wireless Mobile Device (WMD) Overuse Impact Our Physical and Mental Health?

The issue is not how much time is spent on the screens,
but what else could have happened during that time.
—**Nidhi Gupta**

I was born and raised in India. After 16 years of medical education across two different continents, I earned the privilege of being a pediatric endocrinologist—a specialty that diagnoses and treats hormone-related health conditions in children. My first encounter with anything close to a cell phone was during medical school. This *cell phone* was about 5 inches long and 2 inches wide with an additional 1-inch-long antenna sticking out on top. Quite the clunky contraption by today's standards!

I had just graduated from medical school when Apple introduced their first iPhone on January 9, 2007. To this date, I am grateful to Apple for delaying the launch of the iPhone until after my graduation because goodness knows how things would have unfolded otherwise. While Apple's iPhone was certainly not the first smartphone, its user-friendly interface and intuitive features launched a revolution in the technology and communication industries. This was followed by the introduction of the Android operating system a year later, and then the first iPad in April 2010.

By 2017–2018, I began noticing a precipitous increase in the side effects of excessive screen time in my pediatric endocrinology patients, not just from a medical standpoint but also from a social etiquette standpoint. I recall multiple office visits where I would walk into the patient's exam room only to find all family members bent over their wireless mobile devices, parents as well as their children, blissfully unaware that a stranger had joined them. A little throaty noise was usually enough to bring the quorum to attention.

One such visit involved Gabriella, a 14-year-old girl, who looked up from her latest WMD as I entered the exam room. I was meeting the family for the first time due to concerns about Gabriella's excessive weight gain and prediabetes. Prediabetes, if not addressed in a timely fashion, can progress to type 2 diabetes mellitus, a condition linked with grave health impacts.

Gabriella's 8-year-old brother sat in a corner, comfortably engrossed in his own iPad for the entire 45 minutes we spent together. I didn't hear a peep from him; maybe this was the new definition of a *well-behaved child*. Their mom clutched her own WMD protectively, tapping the screen repeatedly to keep it from locking while hastily answering my questions. I was taken aback by Gabriella's flat affect and minimal communication with her mother. I was equally troubled by the condescending nature of the mother's remarks toward her daughter.

During our conversation about lifestyle habits, Gabriella informed me that she had no time after school and homework for physical activity. She was not interested in any after-school activities and spent most of her evenings alone in her room. As the discussion warmed up, she confessed to spending four to five hours each day on her WMD, scrolling through social media, chatting with friends, and watching YouTube videos, but assured me, "I never post anything though."

This revelation finally caught Gabriella's mom's attention, and she looked up, visibly deflated. Through tears, she said, "It's all our fault. We bought her the phone so that she has everything that we did not have back home in Mexico. We did not want her to feel deprived like we did growing up."

It hit me: in trying to give our children the best, we may unintentionally expose them to hidden risks that affect their well-being.

Many young people today struggle to balance screen use with essential activities like exercise, sleep, and face-to-face interactions. In 2010, Sisson *et al.*[61] proposed the *displacement hypothesis*, suggesting that "with a finite number of discretionary hours in a day, physical activity could be displaced or substituted by screen-based sedentary behavior." Nearly a decade later, the displacement hypothesis seems more relevant than ever.

Building upon the displacement hypothesis, I have observed that screen time does more than just take away from physical activity—it serves as an emotional escape. This led me to develop the *Escape-Displace Theory*. This theory posits that "with a finite number of discretionary hours in a day, essential activities of healthy living are often displaced or substituted by screen-based leisurely pursuits." This behavior not only consumes valuable time but also serves as an escape mechanism from coping with negative or challenging real-life situations.[34]

ESCAPE

*Common cues that drive
our escape to WMDs*

- BOREDOM
- EMOTIONAL CONFLICT
- STRESS AND OVERWHELM
- MENTAL FATIGUE OR EFFORT
- PROCRASTINABLE TASK
- PHYSICAL ACTIVITY

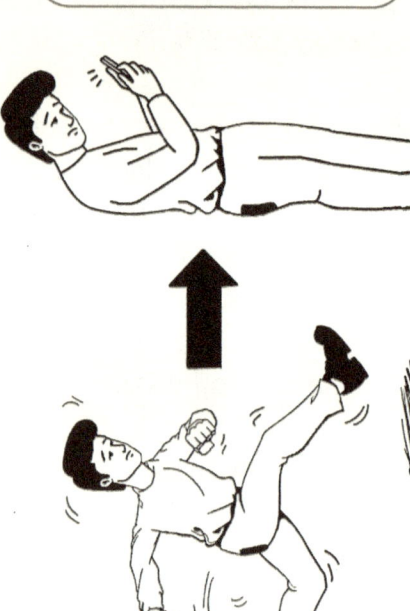

DISPLACE

*Essential activities that are
displaced by WMD overuse*

- EXERCISE
- UNINTERRUPTED MEALS
- SLEEP
- FOCUSED WORK
- LEARNING
- RELATIONSHIPS
- FAMILY TIME
- ATTENTIVE DRIVING

Individuals use WMDs to avoid feelings of boredom, stress, anxiety, and effort (both physical and mental). In doing so, they unintentionally displace essential activities such as physical activity, sleep, and study time. As a result, health issues like obesity, sleep disorders, and mental health problems begin to emerge.

To understand how this plays out in real life, I asked a group of high school students during a seminar, *"What do you escape from?"* Almost in unison, they answered, *"Boredom."*

I prodded further, *"What do you find boring?"*

Their answers came swiftly:

"Assignments."
"Studying."
"Chores."
"Waiting for my turn."
"Slow internet."
"Grocery shopping."
"Being stuck in traffic."
"Waiting for the doctor."

(It was hard not to take that last one personally!)

I continued, *"What else do you escape from?"*

It felt as if a dam had broken. The students candidly shared:

"Emotional conflicts."
"Stress from school."
"Anxiety about grades."
"Math assignments."
"Project deadlines."
"Family arguments."

We dissolve ourselves in the virtual world to escape from pain and discomfort.

Their responses shed light on a broader issue: Coping strategies have been increasingly outsourced to WMDs. We dissolve ourselves in the virtual world to escape from pain and discomfort. The internet numbs the pain for a few minutes, but does the pain truly go away? Of course not—it waits patiently for us to address it, growing heavier the longer we delay.

Our devices are always there to help us *escape* from boring, mundane, or strenuous tasks. But in doing so, we unknowingly displace essential activities that are necessary for our wellness. Let's examine how WMD overuse directly impacts our health:

Weight gain

In a large study of U.S. youth aged 6–17 years old, spending more than two to three hours per day on screen-based leisure activities doubled the odds of becoming overweight.[54] Interestingly, this was back in 2010 when screen time mainly referred to television and video games. Fast-forward a decade, and our screens have literally moved from the living room walls into the palms of infants, toddlers, children, and adults.

There is a clear connection between screen time and weight gain, and it does not boil down just to physical inactivity. Screen time can influence diet by exposing us to food marketing,[62] distracting us into mindless overeating,[63] and even impacting our appetite and feelings of fullness.[59] And let's not forget the

When it's a choice between exercising or scrolling through the latest doom and gloom on the internet, exercise might not stand a chance.

post-video game munchies—research shows that after gaming, people tend to eat more than they would if they were just sitting around doing nothing.[64]

On the flip side, kids who spend fewer than two hours in front of screens tend to have better diets. They are more likely to eat regular meals, including fresh fruit and vegetables, and less likely to indulge in sugary drinks and junk food.[65]

Remember, extensive screen time alone may not lead to poor dietary habits and weight gain if it is compensated with healthy behaviors.[66] But here is the catch: Balancing screen time with healthy behaviors takes Herculean willpower. With only so many hours in a day and the constant dopamine pull from the screens, the odds are stacked against healthy behaviors. When it's a choice between exercising or scrolling through the latest doom and gloom on the internet, exercise might not stand a chance. But if it does, the game of digital wellness has been won!

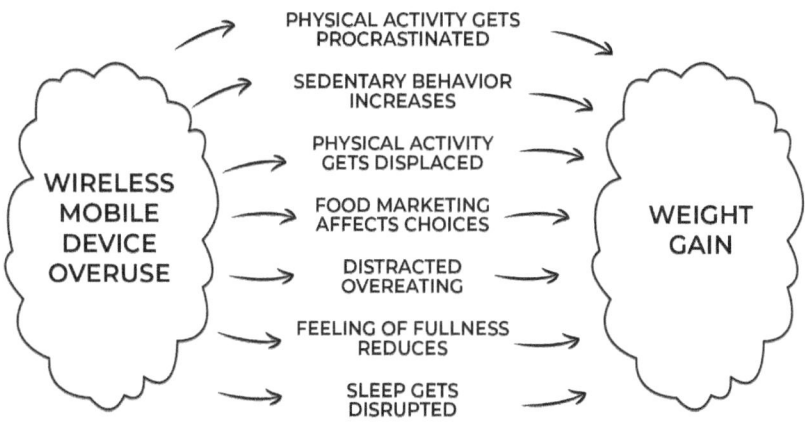

How WMD overuse leads to weight gain

Sleep disorders

Screen time is a major culprit in the epidemic of poor sleep, and it is not just because we stay up too late watching short videos. First, there is the displacement effect—more time on screens means less time for sleep.[61,67] Then there is the addictive nature of our devices and the fear of missing out that prevents us from turning off the screens, even when we know we should be sleeping.[66]

But that's not all. The content we consume on our WMDs—whether it's a heated social media debate or a cliffhanger episode of our favorite show or game—can leave us too wired to fall asleep and stay asleep.

Finally, there is also the issue of blue light. Our screens are lit by light-emitting diodes (LEDs), which emit a lot of blue light—great for keeping screens thin and sharp, but not so great for sleep. Blue light tricks our brains into thinking it's still daytime, suppressing melatonin production, and making it harder to fall asleep.[68] Over time, excessive exposure to blue light could even contribute to age-related macular degeneration.[69,70] So, if you are handing your toddler a WMD before bed, please pause and reevaluate.

The National Sleep Foundation's 2011 Sleep in America Poll found that nine out of ten Americans use a technology device during the hour just before bedtime.[68] The more interactive the device—think smartphones, laptops, or video games—the harder it was to fall asleep or wake up feeling refreshed. Fast-forward to their 2020 poll, and Americans were now feeling sleepy three days a week on average, with sleep deprivation impacting their moods, productivity, and overall sense of well-being. Those who indulge in screen time before bed are more likely to carry extra weight, suffer from dry eyes, and perform poorly at work.[71]

Interestingly, just having a WMD in the bedroom, even if it is not being used, is associated with worse sleep outcomes.[72] Back in 2013, bedtime screen use was found to cut sleep time by 20–45 minutes. Imagine how much worse it is now, with WMDs in 84 percent of U.S. households and technology becoming ever more portable and pervasive.[73–75] And let's be honest, who hasn't been tempted to watch *just one more episode* when the last one ends on a cliffhanger?

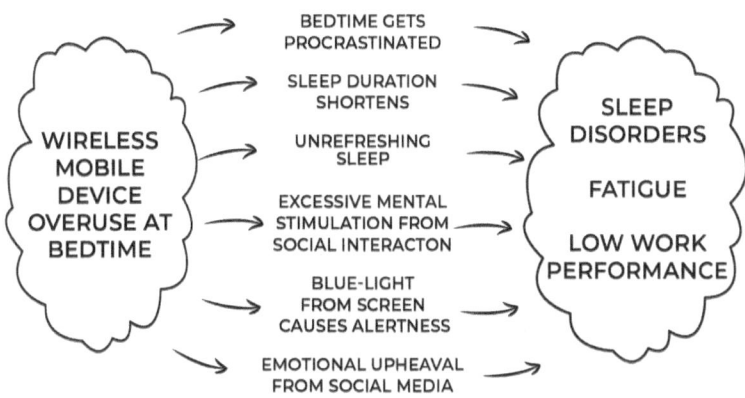

How WMD overuse leads to sleep disorders

Mental health disorders

Extensive screen time and low levels of physical activity interact to increase anxiety, depression, and dissatisfaction with life.[21,29,76,77] In adolescents, these factors contribute to dissatisfaction with school[78] and low self-esteem.[79] The results of a study that included more than 2,500 Chinese college freshmen revealed that more than two hours of screen time per day was associated with higher odds of anxiety, depression, and other psychological issues.[80]

While WMDs are supposed to keep us connected, their overuse can lead to increased isolation in real life.[81] Why does this happen? Here are several possible explanations:

- **Social media replaces face-to-face interactions:** The more time spent online, the less time there is available for real-world connections.[15,16]
- **WMDs are distracting during face-to-face interactions:** Even when we are together with others, our devices keep us from fully engaging, thus dulling the positive effects of social interaction.[82]
- **Ubiquitous WMD presence:** Constant access to WMDs increases the risk of internet addiction and excessive gaming.[83]
- **Sleep disruption:** Poor sleep, as we discussed earlier, can have a negative impact on mental health.[84]
- **Displacement of physical activity:** Vigorous exercise releases mood-lifting endorphins—something WMDs can't do.[85]
- **Social comparison:** On social media, we often compare ourselves to others who seem to have perfect lives, leading to feelings of inadequacy.[86,87]
- **Reinforcing spirals theory:** Algorithms feed us content that reinforces our existing beliefs and interests, keeping us in a filter bubble that can exacerbate anxiety and depression.[29,88]

In 2016, results from a large national sample of U.S. children aged 2–17 revealed that the more time kids spent on screens, the worse their psychological well-being was. After just one hour a day, increasing screen time was linked to less curiosity, lower self-control, more difficulty making friends, diminished emotional stability, and more arguments with caregivers.

Children who spent more than seven hours a day on screens were more likely to consult a mental health professional, be diagnosed with anxiety or depression, and take medication for psychological issues.[89]

And, as if these issues were not enough, there is another very dark side to social media: Explicit images of self-harm can be easily accessed, sometimes with fatal consequences. Over the past decade, social media use facilitated by WMDs has been found to be highly predictive of suicide risk in young adults.[90]

Finally, increased screen time has been linked to riskier behaviors, including substance use, alcohol consumption, smoking, violence, and dangerous sexual behavior.[91] The more time spent on screens, the higher the risk. Some researchers suggest that excessive screen time may lead to anhedonia—the reduced ability to experience pleasure—which in turn might drive people to seek out more extreme stimuli, including drugs or risky behaviors.[45]

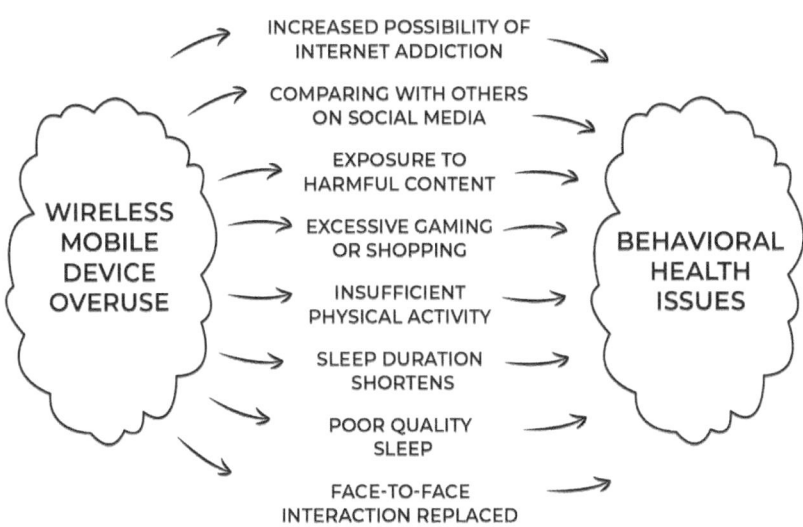

How WMD overuse leads to mental health disorders

Additional compelling data to support these associations are available as part of my research article on this subject, which can be found under the Resources section at calmthenoise.info.

To prevent the downward spiral of escape-displace, you need to shift your mindset to *engage-replace*. The next time you find yourself reaching for your WMD, pause and ask yourself, "Am I picking up my WMD to escape-displace a boring or difficult task? Am I just procrastinating? Am I avoiding something?"

If the answer to any of these questions is yes, pause before reacting. Be kind to yourself, let go of guilt or judgment, and recognize the moment for what it is—an automatic reflex. Reward yourself for catching it. Then, instead of succumbing to the reflex, *engage* actively with the task or person in front of you. By doing this, you start to *replace* (meaning, *put back*) the displaced, meaningful activities that have slowly disappeared from your life.

Returning to Gabriella's story, our discussion sparked a critical shift in her family's approach to technology use. Together, they implemented several changes:

- **Screen-free mealtimes:** The family committed itself to keeping all devices away from the dining table, instead using this time to engage in meaningful conversations.
- **Reducing time-consuming apps:** They evaluated and deleted apps that consumed an excessive amount of time without adding real value to their lives.
- **Traditional alarm clocks:** Replacing WMDs with analog alarm clocks helped eliminate the temptation of late-night screen use and improved their sleep quality.
- **Incorporating physical activities:** Gabriella enrolled in a dance class, and the family started taking evening walks together, turning exercise into a shared and enjoyable experience for all.

- **Non-WMD rewards:** To celebrate achievements and special occasions, the family began choosing rewards that encouraged real-world engagement, including books, art supplies, and outdoor adventures.

While the time I spent with Gabriella's family that day was brief, it ignited their journey toward healthier habits and improved well-being. A few months later, Gabriella returned for a follow-up appointment. She had lost weight, her blood sugar levels were within normal ranges, and most importantly, her confidence and zest for life had visibly increased. Her mother beamed with pride as she shared stories of their family hikes and Gabriella's newfound love for dance. The screens were still a part of their lives, but they no longer dictated their daily routines. In other words, they had found balance.

DELETE THE CUES

Instead of   *Screen-free meal times*

CURB THE CRAVING

Instead of   *Reduce time-consuming apps*

 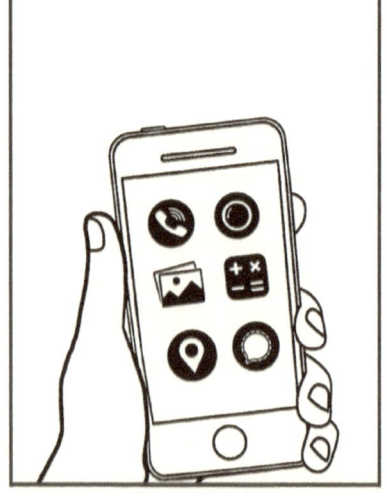

WEAKEN THE RESPONSE

Instead of

Reduce temptation of bedtime screen use

DULL THE REWARD

Instead of

Turn exercise into an enjoyable experience

Your Actionable Recap

- We often use WMDs to escape discomfort, but in doing so, we displace essential healthy activities.
- Excessive screen time leads to sedentary lifestyles, weight gain, and associated health issues like prediabetes and obesity.
- The blue light and stimulation from screens interfere with natural sleep patterns, resulting in poor sleep quality and fatigue.
- Overuse of WMDs, especially social media, has been linked to increased anxiety, depression, and feelings of isolation.

Yes, but ... What if ... How about?

- **Yes, but how do I expect my adolescent to understand these complex concepts?**
  Understandably, these concepts can seem complex, especially for adolescents. The key is to break them down into relatable terms and examples that resonate with their daily experiences.

  Start by discussing the immediate effects of screen time, for example, how staying up late on their phone might make them feel tired and cranky the next day and affect their school performance;[92] or how too much time on social media can lead to feelings of stress or over-comparison. Encourage open conversations where they can share their thoughts and ask questions. You can also set an example by modeling balanced screen use yourself. Remember, resisting the new culture of always being *on* might seem futile, but surrender would be worse.

- **What if my child, who does not own a WMD, checks out stuff on their friend's WMD?**
  Even if your child doesn't own a WMD, it is natural for them to be curious and use their friends' devices. The key here is to have an open dialogue about what they are seeing and experiencing on those devices. Discuss the importance of balance and encourage them to be mindful of how much time they are spending on screens, even if they do not own these devices themselves. You can also talk to the parents of their friends in an effort to align on screen time boundaries during visits.

- **How about managing screen time during sleepovers, especially if the other families are not on board?**
  Managing screen time during sleepovers can be tricky, especially if other families have different rules. One approach is to set clear expectations with your child before the sleepover, discussing how much screen time is reasonable and what other fun activities they can enjoy instead. You might also suggest bringing board games, crafts, or outdoor activities to keep everyone engaged.

  If possible, communicate with the other parents about your preferences, emphasizing that the goal is to ensure the kids have a great time without being glued to their screens. Ultimately, it's about teaching your child to make mindful choices even when you are not around.

Because the brain is not fully developed to exercise self-control until one's mid-20s, it is naturally hard for young people to be disciplined in the face of temptations.

10
How Do Digital Distractions Fuel Burnout?

You will never reach your destination if you stop
and throw stones at every dog that barks.
—**Winston Churchill**

Ronald is a sales representative in his mid-30s. At 8 a.m., he settled at his desk to begin his heavily scheduled workday, his wireless mobile device (WMD) resting peacefully by his arm. By lunchtime, he needed to write a proposal for a prospective client and return three calls from existing clients. He began working on the proposal. Two minutes into this task, his WMD dinged. Habitually, Ronald reached out to find a message from his wife about dinner plans for the weekend. Ronald replied to her but couldn't help getting sidetracked by two other unread notifications on the home screen of his WMD: an update from his news app, and new content on his social media feed.

Ronald proceeded to browse through everything. By this time, he had lost a precious 32 minutes and his train of thought. He tried to gather his attention, worked hastily through the proposal, and managed to send it to the client.

Well ... now Ronald felt *entitled* to take a break. He reached for his WMD again because that's how he had always taken a break! He wanted to get his *mind off things*. So, he played Candy

Crush Saga and Wordle, scrolled again through the news app, moved over to the messages, and took one final look through all the social media feeds. He felt relaxed, updated, and ready to resume work. Or did he?

In fact, Ronald felt tired, scattered, and anything but calm. He was unable to make time for the rest of his work. He decided to procrastinate and ultimately left these pending tasks for after lunch.

Ronald's experience is not unique. His struggle with distractions is shared by employees across industries. The illustration here captures the reality of a distracted employee—someone whose workday is repeatedly hijacked by their WMD, leading to fragmented attention and growing exhaustion.

The results of a 2018 study by Udemy revealed that 70 percent of employees admit to feeling distracted at work, with emails and texts being the primary culprits.[4] We know that it takes about 19–25 minutes to get back on task after being distracted.[3] An average American accesses information on their WMD approximately 96–206 times per day or once every three to six minutes during their waking hours. Imagine the amount of time lost when an employee is distracted 96–206 times a day. This time to recover (about 11 hours of lost productivity each week) can significantly impact an employee's ability to complete tasks efficiently and effectively. Frequent WMD users compensate for the time lost by working faster and cutting corners, leading to more stress and higher levels of frustration.[93,94]

How does workplace distraction translate into revenue loss? Workplace distractions cost U.S. businesses a staggering $588 billion per year.[95] This financial loss includes the time spent on distractions and the effort required to refocus on work after an interruption.

Employees seem to live in a state of constant stimulation, busyness, and distraction.

Employees seem to live in a state of constant stimulation, busyness, and distraction. They do not see these distractions as interruptions to their job. In fact, dealing with frequent interruptions, more commonly known as *multitasking*, seems to become the job.

Typically, an interrupted task is not resumed immediately in about 23–45 percent of the situations, therefore promoting further procrastination and redundancies as the person tries to reorient to the work at some later time.[93] Eventually, the tasks pile up and are then perceived as overwhelming, leading to constant stress over unfinished work.

The purpose of work-related apps and other technological advances was to increase efficiency and productivity, and to allow employees to provide timely and efficient services, wherever and whenever they wanted. The evolution of the work environment has increased the mobility and multitasking abilities of employees, while simultaneously increasing the expectations placed on them.

Beyond distractions, the modern work environment has essentially placed employees, irrespective of their profession, *on call* all the time. Unlike the old-fashioned landline, the WMD is rarely inaccessible. Therefore, the modern-day employee is always reachable and the boundaries between work and life blur.

WMD use in professional settings presents both opportunities and challenges. While WMDs allow an employee to answer emails from their child's playground or during vacation, they can also be a source of distraction and displacement of essential tasks. Concerns have been raised regarding the negative implications of frequent WMD use at work and the obvious addictive nature of these devices.

The higher the perceived difficulty or boredom associated with a task, the higher the odds of displacing it with WMD use.

As discussed in the previous chapters, WMD overuse affects sleep, increases reaction time, reduces work performance, and impairs cognitive abilities. A WMD user might become so engrossed with its content that they choose to displace or procrastinate, thereby avoiding the primary task at hand. The higher the perceived difficulty or boredom associated with a task, the higher the odds of displacing it with WMD use.[11] WMD users can easily lose track of time, be unaware of their own WMD misuse, and fail to realize that they are distracted.

Interruptions from WMD use during a task that requires focused attention also result in a 2.8-fold increase in the chances of error. This can be particularly problematic in certain professions, such as medicine.[96–99] As Daniel Rosenfield, MD at the University of Toronto (Ontario), aptly described the modern-day hospital work environment, "One would be hard-pressed to find a healthcare team in which at least one member is not engaged on their WMD during patient discussion. While they attend to the flashing light or the fancy ringtone, others are usually wondering if they are looking up a life-saving dose of a medicine, answering a text regarding dinner plans, or simply being rude."[100,101]

My full research article discussing the pitfalls of the use of WMDs by healthcare professionals and its association with distraction, errors, procrastination, and burnout is available under the Resources section at calmthenoise.info

Several organizations have imposed restrictions on access to websites, including social media, shopping, and personal emails on institutional computers. While these measures might be effective in safeguarding privacy and security, most employees have access to this content on their WMDs. As one employee who attended our workshop stated, "My WMD is right there—no one could stop me from shopping online if I wanted to."

WMD applications are designed to be more intuitive, user-friendly, and addictive than standard web browsers. It's no wonder that we are often tempted to reach for our WMD when we should not.

It is unclear whether WMD notifications that contain work-related information are as disruptive as those conveying personal messages.[93] For instance, would a text or email from the boss that matched the task at hand (e.g., arranging a team meeting) create as much of a workflow interruption as one that was purely personal? Although one might not actively spend time on such notifications, engaging with a WMD can mentally distract us, leading to decreased productivity and increased stress.

At my visit to Ronald's business for a seminar, he described what seemed like complete energy depletion and burnout. In his book, *Stop Physician Burnout: What to Do When Working Harder Isn't Working*, Dr. Dike Drummond described burnout as the depletion of three energy accounts:[102]

- **Physical:** Feelings of exhaustion due to lack of sleep, healthy nutrition, and exercise.
- **Emotional:** Increased mental distance from one's job or feelings of negativism or cynicism related to one's job.
- **Spiritual:** Reduced professional efficacy, compassion fatigue, and a diminished sense of purpose and meaning in work and life.

Excessive WMD use frequently displaces physical activity, sleep, and face-to-face interactions with friends and colleagues. These patterns have the potential to lead to an even higher risk of burnout, especially considering the inherently stressful nature of the modern workplace.

A week later, I received an email from Ronald:

Dear Dr. Gupta,

I feel like I can go on forever about all the wonderful things that have happened since your seminar, ReConnect. I left the event feeling so grounded and so much more aware of all the sights and smells around me.

I have blocked all social media on my work computer and deleted social media apps from my WMD. I cleaned our house. My wife and I cooked together and went for a screen-free walk after dinner.

The three hours at ReConnect were probably one of the best three hours of my life. Now, I see technology as a tool, and once again have peace of mind while maintaining a high level of productivity.

Thank you!!
Ronald

Your Actionable Recap

- Frequent distractions from WMDs lead to procrastination, reduced productivity, and ultimately, burnout.
- The blur between personal and professional notifications can scatter an employee's attention and contribute to stress and exhaustion.
- Excessive WMD use depletes our physical, emotional, and spiritual energy accounts, leading to burnout.
- Frequent WMD users compensate for the time lost by working faster and cutting corners, leading to errors, stress, and job dissatisfaction.

Yes, but ... What if ... How about?

- **Yes, but if I do not respond to emails and texts right away, people think I am *not invested enough*.**
  Being always available should not be the norm. Sure, it's tempting to be the boss's favorite who responds in seconds, but over time, this *always-on-call* culture can lead to job dissatisfaction and high turnover rates. The key is to have an open dialogue with your colleagues and leaders about updating workplace expectations. Setting clear guidelines and boundaries around digital communication is crucial. Agreeing on what is truly urgent and the best way to handle it will help streamline workflow and create a healthier work-life balance for everyone.

  On a personal level, designate a specific time of the day to check and respond to emails and messages, and make sure to establish clear boundaries so that you do not end up working after hours because you have spent too much time responding to non-urgent work communications.

- **What if I have already started feeling burned out? Can reducing WMD use really help?**
  Yes, reducing your WMD use can be a game changer in combating burnout. When you cut back on screen time, you will free up mental space for activities that nurture your physical (exercise, healthy eating, sleep), emotional (positive outlook on work), and spiritual (passion for your work) buckets.

  A highly distracted mind often turns into an exhausted, scattered, inefficient gooey mess with no capacity for feedback or empathy. Over time, your buckets are drained, leaving you with little to give back to your work, family, or community. Discontentment and dissatisfaction settle in, and before you know it, burnout has taken root.

  Reducing WMD use helps you reclaim your bandwidth and refill your buckets, so you can function at your best, both at work and in life.

- **How about utilizing a separate WMD for work and personal use?**
  On the surface, this strategy sounds like a great idea, but let's dig a little deeper. Can you really use the work WMD strictly for that purpose, turn it off after hours, and resist the urge to carry it around with you like a security blanket? If the answer is yes, then go for it! But if you find yourself constantly syncing notifications between both

devices and using the work WMD for non-work-related activities, then it might have just become a second piece of technology cluttering your life.

In my experience, the work WMD often morphs into just another vice, undermining the very balance you were hoping to achieve.

11

How Do Wireless Mobile Devices (WMDs) Make Driving Riskier?

The most dangerous distractions are the ones
you love, but that don't love you back.
—**Warren Buffett**

I came to a stop at a traffic light on one of the busiest roads in Nashville. I do not like this particular traffic light simply because it is timed in such a way that I need to stop there for quite a long time (45 seconds); this interferes with my typical mad rush to destinations. However, recently I enjoyed stopping here because it provided me with the opportunity to observe human behavior.

As I waited for my signal to turn green, I noticed numerous cars whizzing by, driven by people whose eyes were on anything but the road ahead. This included drivers with one hand on the steering wheel and the other swiping their wireless mobile device (WMD) touch screens; drivers with their WMDs precariously settled in the middle of their steering wheels while glancing up and down every few seconds; drivers with their WMDs clutched in between their ear and a hunched-up shoulder; drivers with both hands off the steering wheel typing away; and drivers watching movies on their WMDs through the corners of their eyes. I even saw drivers with multiple WMDs docked on either side of their steering wheels.

As if this was not amusing enough, one day, a rather strange phenomenon occurred in the cars that had stopped on either side of me. For the first 10–20 seconds, these drivers managed to keep their hands on the steering wheels. But as more and more WMD-preoccupied drivers passed by, the stationary drivers on either side of me, as if robotically conditioned to behave this way, reached for their WMDs and began fidgeting, scrolling, and checking. Was boredom a cue here? Most certainly yes! But as I have since discovered, it's more than just boredom that leads to WMD use in this setting.

Behavior sensitization is often expressed in contexts in which a specific cue or stimulus has previously been experienced or imagined.[20] It also reflects an *occasion-setting* type of mechanism. For example, individuals who are used to browsing WMDs while driving or before bedtime are more likely to continue to do so in those settings, irrespective of the adverse impact on sleep or even a potentially fatal outcome (i.e., while driving).

We see the same behavior patterns play out in other settings. Consider the scenario of riding in an elevator. If other people are using their WMDs, it becomes particularly challenging to resist the urge to check yours. Similarly, an employee walking into a meeting while glued to a WMD sets off a chain reaction—soon, everyone else in the room is following suit, and that's the end of small talk and human connection!

Psychologists agree that an individual who is in remission for drug addiction and is required to walk along a street lined with people using the drug is more likely to relapse.[12] Why? Because of the contextual nature of behavior addiction. Simply put, *"monkey see, monkey do!"*

At this point, you might wonder, "What is wrong with scrolling or checking my WMD while waiting at a traffic light, in an elevator, or before a meeting starts?" The issue is that WMDs have come to deny us the joy of being bored. Yes, there is joy in being bored! Boredom is our brain's default mode. Every time we reach for our WMDs as a time-filler, we rob ourselves of the opportunity to reset our brain to this default mode. Boredom breeds new ideas that lead to curiosity and innovation. So yes, by reaching for our WMD in an elevator, we are, in a way, killing innovation.

The issue is that WMDs have come to deny us the joy of being bored.

When it comes to driving, the consequences are of course even more direct and severe. Overwhelming evidence links WMD use while driving with traffic accidents.[103,104] Engaging with WMDs has been associated with distracted driving, increased brake reaction time, reduced headway, and degraded responses to hazards on the road.[105–108]

Data from multiple studies highlight a marked increase in traffic accidents over the past five to seven years, with WMD use being one of the leading contributors. A report from Zendrive based on the analysis of three million drivers who traveled over 5.6 billion miles revealed that drivers used their phones during 88 percent of trips taken in 2018.[109] The report further stated that phone use behind the wheel increased by 10 percent from the previous year, reflecting the growing tendency of drivers to stay digitally connected while driving.

In a National Academy of Sciences-sponsored report, driver distraction was identified as the cause of nearly 70 percent of the

905 crashes included in the dataset.[103] The authors estimated that 36 percent, or 4 million of the nearly 11 million crashes occurring in the United States annually, could be avoided if distractions were eliminated.

According to the National Highway Traffic Safety Administration (NHTSA), in 2020 alone, distracted driving claimed 3,142 lives in the United States, and the NHTSA also noted that WMD use was one of the most prevalent forms of distraction.[110] Similarly, a 2017 study conducted by the American Automobile Association Foundation for Traffic Safety found that nearly 10 percent of all fatal crashes involved distractions from WMDs.[111]

The boredom of sitting idle in a traffic jam, the need to stay informed or entertained, and the easy availability of a WMD to quell these constant desires compound the intense dopaminergic urge to check the WMD. Unfortunately, these microsecond changes in brain chemistry also lower the perceived risk of accidents related to distracted driving.[112-114]

Some drivers begin to feel invincible and are misled into assuming that they are operating their vehicles safely and that accidents happen only to *others*. The driver is distracted when notifications, the glow of the screen, or simply the presence of a WMD displaces the primary role of the driver on the road and instead diverts attention to the perceived urgency or reward of checking the WMD and responding to notifications. Adverse, sometimes fatal consequences can result from such momentary lapses in attention.

Individuals with high WMD dependency are more likely to engage with their WMD while driving. Although they know that such behavior is dangerous, they may still indulge in it, indicating compulsive behavior. Driver distraction is a major contributing factor to crashes, which are a leading cause of death for individuals under 35 years of age in the United States. The most common WMD-related distractive behaviors while driving include:[115]

1. Answering or making calls using the vehicle's hands-free device system
2. Checking to see who is calling without actually taking the call
3. Typing and reading text messages
4. Scrolling through social media posts

While some of these behaviors (#1 and #2) may be considered low risk, they still involve cognitive, visual, and potentially manual distraction if the WMD needs to be unlocked to bypass the *I am not driving* mode or retrieved from a bag or a pocket. Behaviors #3 and #4 significantly compromise the driver's ability to pay adequate attention to the road and respond quickly to unexpected traffic events. These findings are consistent across device types, whether they are numeric keypads or touchscreen WMDs.[116] Pedestrian safety is also undermined by the use of WMDs while crossing the road, due to cognitive distraction.[117]

Before WMDs became ubiquitous, drivers were already juggling various distractions behind the wheel—applying makeup, balancing a coffee mug in one hand, holding a pet behind the steering wheel, adjusting the car's temperature, fiddling with the navigation system, and streaming just the right music, as well as reading, eating, passing snacks to kids in the back seat, or attempting to resolve their petty arguments. While these types of distractions still exist, the introduction of WMDs and the lack of traffic laws curbing their use, has added a new and far more dangerous layer of distraction that has a significant impact on road safety.

In fact, WMD use while driving is six times more dangerous than drunk driving. A study from the Virginia Tech Transportation Institute showed that drivers take their eyes off the road for an average of five seconds when checking their WMDs; at 55 miles per hour, this is enough time to cover the length of a football field.[118] While other distractions (e.g., adjusting the air conditioning or handing a snack to a child) require only brief moments of lapsed attention, WMD use often results in prolonged disengagement from the road. The cognitive, visual, and manual demands of texting, scrolling, or even talking on the phone can create sustained lapses in focus, leading to devastating consequences.

In fact, WMD use while driving is six times more dangerous than drunk driving.

Here are a few strategies that you may find useful on the road.

- Before starting to drive, check everything that needs to be checked.
- Reinforce this message to yourself: *I am a safe driver. My WMD can wait.*
- Remind yourself: *Each time I reach for my WMD, my children in the back seat are getting a message that this is a normal thing to do.*
- Enable the *driving mode* setting which mutes incoming notifications, except phone calls.

- Use the *driving auto-reply* setting. This might help relieve the textiety of both the driver and the sender.
- Avoid multitasking with WMDs while driving.
- Resist the urge to quickly check your WMD at a traffic light or a stop sign.
- Turn off the display of new text on your vehicle's navigation screen to minimize distraction and reduce textiety.
- Create a playlist of favorite songs ahead of time to prevent the need to navigate WMD to select the next best song while driving.

As the signal turned to green, I heard angry honks from behind as the drivers of my neighboring cars were jolted out of their WMD-induced trances, abruptly ending their selfie-taking or doomscrolling, and bringing their attention back to the road. I drove away feeling concerned about the safety of our roads, our community, and our minds.

CALM THE NOISE WHILE DRIVING

DELETE THE CUES

Instead of   *Check everything before driving*

CURB THE CRAVING

Instead of   *Remind yourself*

WEAKEN THE RESPONSE

Instead of   *Make WMD hard to reach*

DULL THE REWARD

Instead of   *Turn safe driving into a life skill*

Your Actionable Recap

- Behavior addiction is often context-driven—if you are used to browsing your WMD while driving, you are likely to continue doing so in that setting.
- Watching other drivers engage with their WMDs increases the urge to check yours.
- Fatal consequences can result from even a microsecond lapse in attention.
- Typing and reading text messages, along with scrolling through social media, are among the most dangerous of the driver distractions.

Yes, but ... What if ... How about?

- **Yes, but what if I only check my WMD at red lights and stop signs? Isn't that safe?**
  Although you might feel safer, checking your WMD at red lights and stop signs can still lead to dangerous habits. It distracts you from being fully aware of your surroundings and primes you to continue checking it when you start driving again, just to finish that half-typed text or email. Traffic situations can change quickly at stop signs, and even a momentary lapse in attention can cause an accident. Those few seconds on your WMD can delay your reaction when the light turns green or when it's your turn to proceed from the stop sign. This puts you and others at risk.

- **What if I use hands-free options? Isn't that enough to keep me safe?**
  Hands-free devices may reduce some manual distractions, but they still involve cognitive and visual distractions. Your brain is juggling multiple tasks, which can slow your reaction time and impair your judgment. The safest practice is to minimize all WMD use while driving, hands-free or not. After all, it's a matter of life-or-death.

- **How about turning off notifications while driving? Wouldn't that help?**
  Absolutely! Turning off notifications while driving is a great way to reduce distractions. It removes the temptation to check your WMD when you hear that familiar ding or see the screen light up. For even greater safety, consider using the driving mode that automatically silences notifications and sends auto-replies, letting people know you are on the road.

Part 5
The What

12

What Can Be Done to Apply These Ideas to Our Families?

Children have never been very good at listening to their elders, but they have never failed to imitate them.

—**James Baldwin**

In September 2023, our nonprofit organization, Phreedom Foundation, led a weekend digital reset retreat in the serene state park of Natchez Trace, Tennessee. Thirty individuals ranging from 2 to 72 years of age participated in this event. A few weeks before the retreat, Gracie and her mother visited my clinic for a follow-up appointment for Gracie's type 1 diabetes mellitus.

During the appointment, Gracie's mother expressed curiosity about the retreat. Knowing how much time Gracie spent on Roblox and YouTube, I encouraged them to attend. Her mother seemed interested but hesitant. She turned to Gracie and asked, *"Do you think Daddy would come to the retreat?"*

Without a moment's hesitation, 11-year-old Gracie replied, *"Never!"*

Gracie's response speaks volumes about family dynamics in a world where wireless mobile devices (WMDs) have rewired not just children, but first, adults. Parents, with their constant emails, notifications, and social media updates, were among the early adopters of this technology's addictive patterns. Children, being natural imitators, followed suit.

Research confirms this. Exposure to a highly digitalized environment at home adversely affects the physical and mental health of all family members.[119,120] At home, the absence of rule-setting practices, the presence of multiple WMDs, and prolonged parental screen time are all associated with excessive screen time in children.[121] In other words, parents' screen use is a strong predictor of a child's screen habits.[122]

When parents justify their after-hours WMD use as *work-related or decompressing after a long day,* children notice. They see it, understand it, and unfortunately, feel it. They feel ignored, unimportant, and disconnected. Over time, the message becomes clear: The glowing screen holds more value than moments shared with them.

There is no way to convince children that this is simply not the case when they see that their parents are engrossed in a completely separate world, and when they recognize that their parents seem to enjoy this world more than the moments spent together to the point where they refuse to let go.

When nothing else works, the child throws tantrums to get the parents' attention.

Eventually, parents may feel overwhelmed by their child's demands for attention and resort to the simplest solution— giving the child their own WMD. The results are immediate: Silence fills the house as every member of the family retreats into a separate digital bubble. This temporary peace comes at a significant cost—it plants the seeds for lifelong dependency and disconnection.

So far, we have explored dopamine, the anticipation hormone that keeps us hooked

This temporary peace comes at a significant cost—it plants the seeds for lifelong dependency and disconnection.

on the endless scroll of notifications, videos, and reels. But what counters this dopamine-driven cycle? Consider serotonin, a hormone that might be considered dopamine's quiet, stabilizing counterpart.

Serotonin, often called *the happiness hormone,* is released during moments of real-life connections. It flourishes when we engage in activities like laughing with loved ones, playing a game with our children, or taking a walk in nature. Unlike dopamine, which creates a craving for more, serotonin provides lasting contentment and emotional balance.

[**Full disclosure:** While serotonin is essential for emotional well-being, excessive levels often caused by some medications can lead to serotonin syndrome, a serious condition with symptoms that include agitation, confusion, and rapid heart rate.]

When families prioritize serotonin-enriching experiences—device-free dinners, shared outdoor adventures, or bedtime storytelling—they minimize the need for the dopamine overload associated with WMDs. In addition to its biochemical impact on the brain, this imbalance between dopamine and serotonin can alter the very fabric of family relationships.

When children feel unseen and unvalued due to their parents' distraction, they retreat into their own digital worlds, further reducing the opportunities for serotonin-enriching activities and interactions. Without this balance, children and adults alike are more susceptible to depression, anxiety, emotional disconnection, and WMD addiction.

As psychologist Terrence Real explains in *I Don't Want to Talk About It: Overcoming the Secret Legacy of Male Depression,* depression can manifest in two forms: either overt or covert.[122] Overt depression is obvious and clinically apparent. By contrast, covert depression is hidden and frequently masked by maladaptive coping mechanisms, including alcoholism, substance use, smoking, gambling, internet addiction, or video gaming. If circumstances lead to prolonged removal of any one of these coping strategies, for example, a weekend digital reset retreat, rehabilitation program, or substance abstinence, the overt depression then surfaces.

Terrence Real argues that the cure for covert depression is bringing it to the surface. This concept applies to WMD addiction as well. Families must determine what came first: depression or WMD addiction. Of similar concern, does this become a vicious cycle in which individuals who are prone to developing depression are more likely to be drawn into WMD overuse, and then their WMD overuse pulls them deeper into the dark hole of depression?

Gracie's story is a poignant example. She watches her father's obsessive WMD use, feels devalued, and turns to her mother for support. Her mother, afraid to voice her concerns to her husband, leaves Gracie feeling even more isolated. Seeking solace, Gracie retreats to her room, immersing herself in Roblox. The dopamine drip begins, soothing her temporarily but deepening her emotional disconnection and WMD dependency.

Is there a way out? Yes, but it requires choosing the harder, more rewarding path of mindful connection over the easier path of collective digital distraction.

Here is your family's road map to digital wellness:

Step 1: Inform colleagues, family, and friends

- Let those around you know about the changes you are making to reduce WMD dependency.
- Setting expectations can help avoid misunderstandings, especially when your response time to messages slows.

- Discuss what constitutes an urgent issue and explain how to reach you during an emergency.
- Encourage family members to join you on this journey but start with your own habits if they aren't immediately on board.

Step 2: Triage your WMDs

- Evaluate how many devices you own and determine their unique purposes.
- If multiple devices serve similar functions, consider setting one aside. For example, if your phone and tablet both manage emails, texts, and streaming, decide if you truly need both.
- Store any redundant devices out of reach for a trial period and observe whether they're genuinely missed.

Step 3: Declutter your WMD

- Uncluttering your WMD is a major step in breaking the trigger loop. This requires careful planning and familiarizing yourself with all the features of your current WMD.
- Delete unnecessary apps, turn off non-essential notifications, and disable enticing features like red badge alerts.
- Familiarize yourself with the steps presented in Chapter 4 to reduce the cues that drive compulsive use.

Step 4: Track your screen time

- Use features like Apple's Screen Time or Android's Digital Wellbeing to monitor your WMD usage.
- While not perfect, these tools provide valuable insights into your habits, including daily pickups, app usage, and notifications.

Daily practices for digital wellness at home:

Bedtime
- Invest in a traditional alarm clock instead of your WMD.
- Avoid installing screens in the bedrooms.
- Stow away all WMDs at least 30–60 minutes before bedtime.
- Skip checking emails or social media before bed.
- If waking up in the middle of the night, avoid checking the WMD.

Morning
- Avoid WMD use for the first 30–60 minutes of your day.
- Engage meaningfully in activities like stretching, hydrating, meditating, exercising, and preparing breakfast.

Meals
- Keep WMDs off the table during meals, both at home and outside the home.

Evenings
- Establish a *WMD basket* for device-free family time.
- Turn off autoplay on streaming platforms to prevent binge-watching.
- Subscribe to a newspaper to minimize reliance on your WMD for news.

Vacations
- Set out-of-office replies for all emails (personal and work).
- Designate proxies for emergencies.
- Plan activities in advance to minimize endless browsing during trips.

Some of the guidance in this chapter might feel repetitious of some of the concepts discussed earlier. This is intentional and is meant to emphasize that they are important. Additionally, some of these suggestions might already be part of your family's routine. My hope is that the insights into how the mind works, combined with actionable strategies, will help you approach these routines with more conviction. For example, if you are one of the rare families in your circle that discourages screen-filled playdates, I hope the ideas in this book empower you to stay the course, even when it feels lonely.

Even when family members resist, taking the first step as an individual can still lead to transformation.

Gracie's family ultimately decided not to attend the retreat. Her mother admitted feeling uncertain about initiating changes when her husband wasn't on board, fearing it would cause more conflict at home.

Months later, Gracie returned for a follow-up visit. This time, she seemed more withdrawn, clutching her WMD even more tightly than before. While her mother expressed continued concerns about Gracie's well-being, she also seemed resigned. *"I don't know what to do anymore,"* she said softly, glancing at her daughter, who was engrossed in her WMD.

This experience was a painful reminder that change often requires collective effort, but it doesn't always need to begin that way. Even when family members resist, taking the first step as an individual can still lead to transformation. Gracie's story lingers with me as a call to action for all of us to lead by example, persist in creating healthier habits, and remember that it's never too late to start.

CALM THE NOISE IN YOUR FAMILY

DELETE THE CUES

Instead of

Device-free evenings

CURB THE CRAVING

Instead of

Screen-free meals

WEAKEN THE RESPONSE

Instead of

Skip WMD for first 30 minutes of your day

DULL THE REWARD

Instead of

Plan trip itineraries in advance

Your Actionable Recap

- Digital wellness begins with adults at home. Lead by example to inspire change in your family.
- Prioritize real-life connections to counter digital dependency.
- Implement practical steps: Declutter WMDs, track screen time, and establish device-free zones.

Yes, but ... What if ... How about?

- **Yes, but what if my partner refuses to change their habits?**
  Start by focusing on your own habits and let your actions speak louder than your words. Over time, your consistency might inspire your partner to join you. If that does not happen, consider exploring what might be driving your partner's WMD dependency. Could it be unresolved trauma, underlying mental health issues (e.g., anxiety or depression), or even certain personality traits?

  A counselor can help navigate these concerns and provide a neutral space to discuss the impact of these habits on your relationship. Hearing your perspective might be the first step toward self-awareness and change.

- **What if my kids resist screen-free time and complain?**
  Resistance is natural at first, especially if excessive screen use has been ingrained over time. Stay patient and consistent. Gradual reduction often works best: reduce screen time in small increments until you reach

a level that aligns with your family's values. To ease the transition, introduce engaging alternatives like board games, outdoor activities, or shared hobbies.

Keep in mind that prolonged screen exposure raises the dopamine threshold for pleasure, making normal activities seem dull in comparison. Counteract this by fostering serotonin-boosting activities like spending time in nature and building real-life human connections. Remember, it is not going to be easy, but it will be worth it!

- **How about occasional indulgence in screens?**
  The answer depends on your definition of *occasional*. For some, it might mean a few hours per day; for others, it could be a family movie night once a week. Moderation is key. Leisure screen time isn't inherently harmful if it doesn't displace essential activities or real-life connections.

  That said, it can be challenging to disembark even briefly from the *dopamine train* once you have hopped on. The pleasure derived from occasional indulgence can make the return to everyday life feel less satisfying and require significant willpower. Realizing that this response is expected and temporary, I suggest setting clear boundaries in advance. This will make success more obtainable and help you avoid getting back on the dopamine train.

13

What Can Be Done to Apply These Ideas in Our Workplaces?

It's not the load that breaks you down;
it's the way you carry it.
—**Lou Holtz**

"I am on a timer!" Anthony lamented as he described his workday. This was his third job this year and, so far, the most stable one. He works at the warehouse of a major online shopping platform, where efficiency, productivity, and focus are key requirements. Wireless mobile device (WMD) use is strictly prohibited during work hours.

Curious, I asked, "How does that work for you?"

Anthony took a deep breath and admitted, "At first, I hated it and didn't think I'd last. But a few weeks in, I found that I actually enjoy being in my own headspace. The structure works for me. I get about 25,000 steps a day, feel healthier not scrolling away all the time, and I'm more present in the moment. Plus, they treat me well."

Anthony's experience highlights how intentional boundaries, even imposed ones, can create a ripple effect on focus and well-being. While this narrative offers only a glimpse into the success of Anthony's workplace, it raises an important question: Could other workplaces benefit from similar strategies?

Workplace distractions are pervasive and costly:

- Seventy percent of employees admit to feeling distracted at work, with emails and texts being the primary culprits.[4]
- It takes about 19–25 minutes to regain focus after being distracted.[3]
- The average American checks their WMD 96–206 times per day, leading to countless interruptions.
- Workplace distractions cost U.S. businesses a staggering $588 billion annually.[95]
- Frequent WMD users compensate for lost time by working faster and cutting corners, which increases stress and frustration.[93,94]

These statistics reveal a startling truth: Workplace distractions are not just inconveniences; they are profound obstacles to productivity, mental health, and job satisfaction.

Optimizing the digital environment at workplaces serves several purposes. Besides the obvious boost in efficiency and productivity, the potential for burnout goes down, and job satisfaction goes up. As we explored in Chapter 10, distractions contribute to burnout. But the opposite is also true: Reducing distractions can increase job satisfaction.

Workplace distractions are not just inconveniences; they are profound obstacles to productivity, mental health, and job satisfaction.

When employees feel empowered to manage digital distractions effectively, they regain control over their time and attention. By creating a more focused and less distracting work setting, more work gets done, which means less work gets taken home. This translates into more time for self-care and for nurturing the serotonin-boosting relationships. Eventually, this leads to greater fulfillment, both at work and at home.

The modern workplace often fosters digital overload. Employees face email anxiety, with inboxes overflowing with hundreds, sometimes thousands of unread emails.[123,124] This is especially challenging for younger employees, even though they grew up in the digital age. Their communication preferences might lean toward instant messaging platforms and social media, which makes the more structured and formal nature of email communications complex for them.

Regardless of age, many workplace emails could be replaced with quick, collaborative team meetings. This approach can reduce digital clutter and foster face-to-face interaction, which boosts team cohesion and morale. However, the key lies in keeping these meetings brief and purposeful. We all have endured 60-minute meetings that could have been resolved with a single email!

Another major challenge is the unspoken expectation of 24/7 availability that can blur the boundaries between work and personal life. The expectations are partly driven by the fear of missing out on opportunities or losing a project, and partly by the pressure to respond immediately to avoid being labeled as uncommitted or unresponsive. However, the relentless connectivity can increase stress and lead to feelings of being constantly tethered to work obligations.

And then there are text messages—those uninvited guests that arrive without notice or appointment, often in overwhelming numbers, completely disrupting the flow of the workday. During my clinics, I make a conscious effort to put my WMD on silent mode and out of sight to avoid being distracted by incoming texts. Yet, as irony would have it, the moment I need my WMD for a two-factor authentication (2FA) code, I get drawn into the flood of notifications on the screen. By the time I finally retrieve the code, it has already expired!

Our relationship with WMDs, particularly in the workplace, hovers between dependency and addiction. When embarking on your digital wellness journey to reduce your reliance on these devices, it is natural to expect to experience withdrawal symptoms such as uneasiness, irritability, fear, restlessness, and anxiety. This process is not linear, and I encourage you to work at a pace that feels comfortable and balances your professional and personal goals.

Recommendations for fostering digital wellness at work will, of course, vary depending on the nature of your occupation. However, many of the suggestions in this chapter are broad enough to apply to a variety of work environments. Use your discretion and tailor these strategies to fit your specific workplace dynamics.

First, begin with the foundational Steps 1–4 outlined in Chapter 12. Once you have incorporated those basics, revisit this chapter for a continued road map to building a distraction-free workplace.

Step 5: Create a mental signboard

- Mentally flip a *closed* sign when your workday ends.
- This intentional shift helps you transition from work mode to personal life mode.

Step 6: Embrace boredom

- Instead of reaching for your WMD during a break, try stretching, hydrating, or sitting in silence.
- Talk to your mind:
  "I know you are bored, but indulging in distractions will not help! Let's reset and refocus instead."

Step 7: Environmental changes

- Limit email access: Delete emails from your smartphone and check them only on a desktop or laptop. While this may seem inconvenient initially, it significantly reduces distractions.
- Remove social media and gaming apps: If not already done in Step 3 (declutter your WMD), now is the time! These apps not only consume time and invite errors, but they also drain your mental energy. Even without workplace rules, let's stay committed to our work, our sense of self, and our wellness.

Daily practices for digital wellness at work:

Managing emails
- Specify times of the day to check emails (e.g., the start and the middle of the day).
- At other times, keep the email window closed to avoid distraction from each new email and the urge to reply instantly.
- Batch process emails and text messages to improve efficiency.[93]
- Unsubscribe from unnecessary email lists to cut down clutter.
- Create separate email accounts for shopping, work, and personal use to streamline notifications.

Managing texts

- Use features such as *Auto-reply* and *Focus* to silence notifications.
- Suggest workflow changes to reduce reliance on texting.
- Don't engage with numbers that send spam texts. Resist replying—even if the text says to reply STOP to opt out. Scammers use any reply as confirmation that your number is active, which could lead to more spam.
- Block numbers that send spam texts.

Optimizing your workspace

- Invest in tools like analog wristwatches and desk calendars to reduce WMD dependency.
- Make WMD hard to reach by putting it away in a desk drawer for 15- to 20-minute intervals.
- Work in uninterrupted 15- to 20-minute blocks, gradually increasing the duration.
- Keep sticky notes handy for jotting down distracting thoughts.
- Keep incoming call notifications on for urgent situations.

Calm the noise

- Actively challenge distracting thoughts through a mental dialogue:

  "I know I am procrastinating, but I will feel better completing this task now without distractions."

  "I am sure nothing has changed on social media or in the news since I checked 15 minutes ago."

  "Any new emails can wait until my designated time to review them."

"If someone needed to reach me urgently, they could always call—my phone's call alerts are on."

"I just verified that my phone's call alert is turned on. There is no need to check it again."

Anthony's journey reminds us that structure and discipline, though initially uncomfortable, can liberate us in ways we never imagined. The no-phone policy at his workplace pulled him out of the whirlpool of digital distractions. By embracing these boundaries, Anthony reclaimed his focus, health, and peace of mind.

While a no-phone policy may not be feasible for every workplace, Anthony's story challenges us to confront our own habits and ask: What boundaries can we create to reclaim our time, attention, and commitment to our workplace?

Anthony's journey reminds us that structure and discipline, though initially uncomfortable, can liberate us in ways we never imagined.

Clearly, when we calm the digital noise, we rediscover the joy of being present, and the ability to put our best foot forward, not just at work, but in life.

Your Actionable Recap

- Workplace distractions are not just inconveniences; they are profound obstacles to productivity, mental health, and job satisfaction.
- Optimizing digital environments in the workplace reduces burnout and increases job satisfaction.
- Take non-digital breaks—stretch, hydrate, or engage in brief, restorative activities.
- Limit email and app access on phones; use desktops for work-related tasks.
- Replace long email threads with quick team meetings to improve clarity and morale.
- Stow away WMDs, use traditional tools (wristwatch, desk calendar), and work in uninterrupted blocks.

Yes, but ... What if ... How about?

- **Yes, but I need my WMD for 2FA.**
  Absolutely, I get it. Accessing your 2FA codes is critical, and your WMD is often the gateway. However, this doesn't mean it has to become a distraction hub. Start by making your WMD less enticing. Turn off non-essential notifications, delete time-consuming apps, and keep it in silent mode except for urgent calls. When it is time to use 2FA, access the code promptly and put the device away before the rabbit hole of distractions sucks you in.

  A bonus tip? Disable biometric unlocking (like facial recognition) and stick to a passcode. The last thing you need is your WMD unlocking itself just because it is happy to *see you* each time you pick it up.

- **What if my job requires constant connectivity?**
  Let's pause and reflect. Does your job truly require constant connectivity, or is this a perception fueled by a fear of missing out? Often, the pressure to check in repeatedly stems from the fear of missing something urgent when, in reality, most things can wait. Start by actively challenging these distracting thoughts with a mental dialogue, as outlined in this chapter: "Is this truly urgent, or can it wait until my scheduled check-in time?"

  Set clear boundaries by designating specific times to check work-related emails and messages. Communicate your availability to your team (and yourself!). Yes, it is natural to feel a part of your brain occupied with thoughts like, "I need to check now," "I cannot wait until my scheduled time," or "A little peek won't hurt anyone." This discomfort will diminish with practice and consistency.

  Remember, staying glued to your WMD doesn't necessarily equate to productivity. It's about working smarter, and not tethering yourself to a screen.

- **How about banning WMDs at work altogether?**
  Let's be honest—what does our workday look like anymore? It has become a multitasking circus. Between juggling household chores (grocery orders, dinner plans, school emails), personal matters (appointments, vacation plans), online distractions (social media, news, reels, short videos, games, shopping), and work responsibilities, it's a wonder we get anything done! So, the question is: Should workplaces step in and impose a *no personal WMD use* policy during work hours?

While such a rule might seem extreme, it could create boundaries that enhance focus and reduce distractions. But here is the catch: Are we ready to accept these rules as the new normal, or have we gone too far in our WMD dependency? Maybe we don't need a full ban but rather a pilot policy—no personal WMD use in certain zones or hours—to see the benefits firsthand. Something to think about!

Conclusion

"His personality seems to have changed. Could that be because of growth hormone?" Jordan's mother asked curiously. I prodded, "Tell me more."

Jordan is 10 years old. A few months ago, I started him on growth hormone treatment for growth hormone deficiency. His mother elaborated that since being on treatment "Jordan has seemed more withdrawn, less communicative, and almost dep ...". She stopped mid-sentence. Jordan interrupted with a mix of anger and disbelief, "Did you just almost say that I'm depressed?"

While I was searching my mental database for possible explanatory side effects of growth hormone, his mother hesitated before adding that Jordan had also received a smart-phone around the same time.

The room fell silent—a silence that spoke louder than any words. It was clear what had caused Jordan's personality changes, but no one dared to verbalize it.

As we dug deeper, it became apparent that Jordan was spending hours watching YouTube and playing video games on his new wireless mobile device (WMD). Late nights on the screen left him disinterested in books, toys, and outdoor play. When I gently educated his parents about the effects of excessive online content on a developing brain, his mother recalled how their older son had struggled with video game addiction—an experience she deeply regretted.

Jordan's father, looking crestfallen, defended his decision: "Well, we had a spare smartphone sitting around at home, and we were paying the bill for it. I thought it might be okay for Jordan to have it for the school bus." His mother had disagreed. By now, she realized that Jordan's mood changes had little to do with growth hormone.

What struck me most was how Jordan's father seemed oblivious to his own dependency on his WMD, a habit he may have unconsciously projected onto his son. He added, "You know, I use my phone all the time—for work, for news, for staying connected. It's just how life is these days. I felt bad seeing Jordan bored when there's so much out there to keep him busy, and all his friends are socializing online anyway." His justification for giving Jordan the WMD mirrored his own underlying anxiety about detaching from his device, which had laid the groundwork for Jordan's tech habits early on.

What followed next was something I often encounter in these situations. All attention turned toward Jordan and how *he* needed to spend less time online, why this was not good for *him*, and how *he* needed to find other things to do. His parents explained to me how there was no one around for him to play with because all the neighborhood kids preferred to socialize online. Jordan sat there with a sullen look, imagining the possibility of losing his new favorite toy. At the same time, he was clueless about why he was being blamed for using something his father had willingly handed to him.

In my 16 years of medical training, I had never imagined that my work in pediatric endocrinology would intersect with digital wellness in such a peculiar way nearly every day. Almost every patient, irrespective of their age, education level, or socio-economic status, seems to be affected by an overindulgence in WMDs. Of course, I cannot engage every endocrine patient in the complexities of digital wellness, given the breadth and depth of the discussion required.

However, these personal and professional encounters reinforce a fundamental truth: Digital wellness begins with adults. There is little doubt that if adults prioritize digital wellness, their children will follow suit. The reshaping of adult minds is leading to tech-addicted generations, and adults must escape digital addiction first to save the next generation.

Much of this reshaping is unintentional, driven by the tech companies and content developers with vested interests in keeping us online. The bright side is that education helps—immensely. Once adults understand the impact of tech on their own and their child's brains, they are compelled to pause and reflect, even if only momentarily.

Change is not immediate or universal. While some individuals transform their habits, others struggle to take the first step. But rarely have I met anyone who denies the science behind tech addiction or its profound impact on physical and mental health.

I encourage you to pause the impulse to follow what you have always done or what everyone else does and find the courage to step away from the cultural norms that are not uplifting you or your family.

Here is why:

- **TIME:** You will save SO much of it. And with that extra time? You will do things—important, sometimes trivial, but always meaningful.
- **NOISE:** You will keep the noise out. Without the constant download of notifications, reels, comments, and memes, your life will feel ... CALM.

Through *Calm the Noise*, I hope to help you see beyond the surface of your relationship with your WMDs. The essential truth is:

The device (WMD) is just the medium. It is merely a tool.
The addiction is not to the device.
The addiction is to the content.
The addiction is to distraction.
The addiction is to the need to avoid boredom.
The addiction is to the feeling of being informed.

Our constant online connectivity is not harmless. It rewires our brains, leading to shorter attention spans and a diminished capacity for deep thinking. In a screen-saturated world, real-life human connection still remains vital, grounding us in ways no digital interaction ever could.

And again, *the issue is not about how much time we spend on screens, but what else could have happened during that time.* What meaningful moments and experiences could have filled those hours? What did we miss?

Nowhere is this loss more apparent than in the workplace. Distractions are not mere inconveniences; they are profound obstacles to productivity, mental health, and job satisfaction. When we allow constant interruptions, we compromise our ability to do our best work and to feel fulfilled by it.

The good news? You do not have to stay trapped in the cycle of digital addiction. The trigger loop (cue, craving, response, reward) can be interrupted at any of these four steps. To kick-start your digital wellness journey, here are the four foundational steps:

1. Turn off non-essential notifications.
2. Physically separate yourself from your WMD for 30–90 minutes daily.

3. Delete time-consuming apps and content.
4. Embrace boredom and allow creativity and focus to thrive.

You might already be familiar with or practicing these steps. Their simplicity might make you doubt their effectiveness. However, the knowledge you have gained from *Calm the Noise* should empower you to implement these changes with conviction. Remember, digital wellness is not about deprivation; it is about reclaiming your time, focus, and ultimately, your life.

Ms. Penny Treese, a talented fine artist, sent this note a few days after she attended our seminar, *ReConnect*. Her words reflect the potential for change and the importance of being intentional toward digital wellness.

June 20, 2022
Dr. Nidhi,

Your insights have forever shifted my thinking regarding WMD use and the effects on me as well as my family, friends, and the world. Change starts with me and I'm already changing my relationship with my devices, for the better. Yet it will take practice and persistence. I have shared your expertise and the ReConnect experience with a few friends in the few short days since your seminar and each time, I'm reminded of what I must do to make profound adjustments in my life.

You are a phenomenal force for good, Dr. Nidhi. I'm blessed and honored to have been an active part of your vision.

With gratitude,
Penny Treese

As we move forward, let's remember that digital wellness is a journey. It requires practice and persistence, but the rewards are profound. Here's to a world where technology enriches rather than engulfs, where every moment counts, and where connection happens in real life, not just online.

Appendix

FOR FURTHER STUDY

Price, C. A. (2018) *How To Break Up With Your Phone. The 30-Day Plan to Take Back Your Life*. Berkeley, CA. Ten Speed Press.

Burke, H. (2019) *The Phone Addiction Workbook. How to Identify Smartphone Dependency, Stop Compulsive Behavior, and Develop a Healthy Relationship with Your Devices*. Brooklyn, NY: Ulysses Press.

Clear, J. (2018) *Atomic Habits*. New York, NY: Penguin Random House.

Sinek, S. (2009) *Start with Why: How Great Leaders Inspire Everyone to Take Action*. New York, NY: Portfolio, Penguin Random House.

Faber, A. and Mazlish, E. (2004) *How To Talk So Kids Will Listen & Listen So Kids Will Talk*, 20th Edition, New York, NY: Harper Perennial.

Covey, S. (1989) *The Seven Habits of Highly Effective People*. New York, NY: Free Press.

Gazaly, A. and Rosen, L. D. (2017) *The Distracted Mind*. Cambridge, MA: MIT Press.

Haidt, J. (2024) *The Anxious Generation*. New York, NY: Penguin Press.

Twenge, J. (2017) *iGen: Why Today's Super-Connected Kids Are Growing Up Less Rebellious, More Tolerant, Less Happy – and Completely Unprepared for Adulthood – and What That Means for the Rest of Us*. New York, NY: Atria Books.

Kamenetz, A. (2018) *The Art of Screen Time. How Your Family Can Balance Digital Media and Real Life*. New York, NY: PublicAffairs.

Murrow, D. (2020) *Drowning in Screen Time. A Lifeline for Adults, Parents, Teachers, and Ministers Who Want to Reclaim Their Real Lives*. New York, NY: Regnery.

Turkle, S. (2012) *Alone Together: Why We Expect More from Technology and Less from Each Other*, 1st Edition. New York, NY: Basic Books.

Duhigg, C. (2012) *The Power of Habit. Why We Do What We Do in Life and Business*. New York, NY: Random House.

References

1. Gupta, Nidhi. "Pitfalls in the Use of Mobile Wireless Devices in Healthcare: Distraction, Errors, Procrastination, and Burnout." *American Journal of Medicine Open* 7 (2022):100010. https://doi.org/10.1016/j.ajmo.2022.100010

2. Gupta, Nidhi. "Impact of Smartphone Overuse on Health and Well-Being Review and Recommendations for Life-Technology Balance." *Journal of Applied Sciences and Clinical Practice* 4(1):4–12, Jan–Apr 2023. https://doi.org/10.4103/jascp.jascp_40_22

3. Mark, Gloria, Daniela Guidth, and Ulrich Klocke. "The Cost of Interrupted Work: More Speed and Stress." *In: Proceedings of the Special Interest Group on Computer-Human Interaction (SIGCHI) Conference on Human Factors in Computing Systems,* Florence, Italy (2008):107–10. https://doi.org/10.1145/1357054.1357072

4. Udemy Business. "Udemy in Depth: 2018 Workplace Distraction Report." Last modified 2018. https://business.udemy.com/resources/udemy-in-depth-2018-workplace-distraction-report/

5. Clear, James. *Atomic Habits: An Easy & Proven Way to Build Good Habits & Break Bad Ones*: Penguin Random House, 2018.

6. Carr, Nicholas. *The Shallows: What the Internet Is Doing to Our Brains*: W. W. Norton & Company, 2010.

7. Jackson, Maggie. *Distracted: Reclaiming Our Focus in a World of Lost Attention*: Prometheus Books, 2008.

8. Wang, Yuxi, Martin McKee, Aleksandra Torbica, and David Stuckler. "Systematic Literature Review on the Spread of Health-related Misinformation on Social Media." *Social Science and Medicine* 240 (2019):112552. https://doi.org/10.1016/j.socscimed.2019.112552

9. Ward, Adrian F., Kristen Duke, Ayelet Gneezy, and Maarten W. Bos. "Brain Drain: The Mere Presence of One's Own Smartphone Reduces Available Cognitive Capacity." *Journal of the Association for Consumer Research* 2, no. 2 (2017):140–54. https://doi.org/10.1086/691462

10. Greenfield, David N. "Treatment Considerations in Internet and Video Game Addiction: A Qualitative Discussion." *Child and Adolescent Psychiatric Clinics of North America* 27, no. 2 (2018):327–44. https://doi.org/10.1016/j.chc.2017.11.007

11. Berridge, Kent C., and Terry E. Robinson. "Liking, Wanting, and the Incentive-Sensitization Theory of Addiction." *The American Psychologist* 71, no. 8 (2016):670–9. https://doi.org/10.1037/amp0000059

12. Hou, Haifeng, Shaowe Jia, Shu Hu, Rong Fan, Wen Sun, Taotao Sun, Hon Zhang. "Reduced striatal dopamine transporters in people with internet addiction disorder." *Journal of Biomedicine and Biotechnology* 2012 (2012):654524.

13. H. S. Seo, E.-K. Jeong, S. Choi, Y. Kwon, H.-J. Park, and I. Kim. "Changes of Neurotransmitters in Youth with Internet and Smartphone Addiction: A Comparison with Healthy Controls and Changes after Cognitive Behavioral Therapy." *American Journal of Neuroradiology* 41 (2020):1293–1301. https://doi.org/10.3174/ajnr.A6632

14. Berridge, Kent C., and Morten L. Kringelbach. "Pleasure Systems in the Brain." *Neuron* 86, no. 3 (2015):646–64. https://doi.org/10.1016/j.neuron.2015.02.018

15. The Lancet. "Social Media, Screen Time, and Young People's Mental Health." *Lancet* 393, no. 10172 (2019):611. https://doi.org/10.1016/S0140-6736(19)30358-7

16. Tromholt, Morten. "The Facebook Experiment: Quitting Facebook Leads to Higher Levels of Well-Being." *Cyberpsychology, Behavior, and Social Networking* 19, no. 11 (2016):661–6. https://doi.org/10.1089/cyber.2016.0259

17. Lu, Hua, James B. Holt, Yiling J. Cheng, Xingyou Zhang, Stephen Onufrak, and Janet B. Croft. "Population-Based Geographic Access to Endocrinologists in the United States, 2012." *BMC Health Services Research* 15 (2015):541. https://doi.org/10.1186/s12913-015-1185-5

18. Grant, Jon E., Murad Atmaca, Naomi A. Fineberg, Leonardo F. Fontenelle, Hisato Matsunaga, Y. C. Janardhan Reddy, Helen B. Simpson, et al. "Impulse Control Disorders and "Behavioural Addictions" in the ICD-11." *World Psychiatry* 13, no. 2 (2014):125–7. https://doi.org/10.1002/wps.20115

19. Chang, Anne-Marie, Daniel Aeschbach, Jeanne F. Duffy, and Charles A. Czeisler. "Evening Use of Light-Emitting Ereaders Negatively Affects Sleep, Circadian Timing, and Next-Morning Alertness." *Proceedings of the National Academy of Sciences* 112, no. 4 (2015):1232–7. https://doi.org/10.1073/pnas.1418490112

20. Kortesoja, Laura, Mari-Pauliina Vainikainen, Risto Hotulainen, and Ilona Merikanto. "Late-Night Digital Media Use in Relation to Chronotype, Sleep and Tiredness on School Days in Adolescence." *Journal of Youth and Adolescence* 52(2023): 419–33. https://doi.org/10.1007/s10964-022-01703-4

21. De-Sola Gutierrez, José, Fernando Rodriguez de Fonseca, and Gabriel Rubio. "Cell-Phone Addiction: A Review." *Frontiers in Psychiatry* 7 (2016):175. https://doi.org/10.3389/fpsyt.2016.00175

22. Grant, Jon E., Marc E. Potenza, Aviv Weinstein, and David A. Gorelick. "Behavioral Addictions: Risk Factors, Diagnosis, and Treatment." *American Journal of Drug and Alcohol Abuse* 36 (2010) 233–241. https://doi.org/10.3109/00952990.2010.491884

23. Robinson, Terry E., and Kent C. Berridge. "The Neural Basis of Drug Craving: An Incentive-Sensitization Theory of Addiction." *Brain Research Reviews* 18, no. 3 (1993):247–91. https://doi.org/10.1016/0165-0173(93)90013-p

24. Robinson, Terry E., and Kent C. Berridge. "The Incentive Sensitization Theory of Addiction: Some Current Issues." *Philosophical Transactions of the Royal Society B* 363, no. 1507 (2008):3137–46. https://doi.org/10.1098/rstb.2008.0093

25. Thalemann, R., K. Wölfling, and S. M. Grüsser. "Specific Cue Reactivity on Computer Game-Related Cues in Excessive Gamers." *Behavioral Neuroscience* 121, no. 3 (2007):614–8. https://doi.org/10.1037/0735-7044.121.3.614

26. Maza, M. T, K. A. Fox, S.-J. Kwon, et al. "Association of Habitual Checking Behaviors on Social Media with Longitudinal Functional Brain Development." *JAMA Pediatrics* 177, no. 2 (2023): 160–7. https://doi.org/10.1001/jamapediatrics.2022.4924

27. Gazzaley, Adam, and Larry D. Rosen. *The Distracted Mind: Ancient Brains in a High-Tech World:* The MIT Press, 2017.

28. Jarius, S., and B. Wildemann. "And Pavlov Still Rings a Bell: Summarising the Evidence for the Use of a Bell in Pavlov's Iconic Experiments on Classical Conditioning." *Journal of Neurology* 262, no. 9 (2015):2177–8. https://doi.org/10.1007/s00415-015-7858-5

29. Boers, Elroy, Mohamma H. Afzali, Nicola Newton, and Patricia Conrod. "Association of Screen Time and Depression in Adolescence." *JAMA Pediatrics* 173, no. 9 (2019):853–9. https://doi.org/10.1001/jamapediatrics.2019.1759

30. United States Centers for Disease Control and Prevention. "Quickstats: Suicide Rates for Teens Aged 15–19 Years, by Sex — United States, 1975–2015." *Morbidity and Mortality Weekly Report* 66 (2017):816. https://doi.org/10.15585/mmwr.mm6630a6

31. Primack, Brian A., Ariel Shensa, Jaime E. Sidani, Erin O. Whaite, Liu Yi Lin, Daniel Rosen, Jason B. Colditz, Ana Radovic, and Elizabeth Miller. "Social Media Use and Perceived Social Isolation among Young Adults in the U.S." *American Journal of Preventive Medicine* 53, no. 1 (2017):1–8. https://doi.org/10.1016/j.amepre.2017.01.010

32. Hunt, Melissa G., Rachel Marx, Courtney Lipson, and Jordyn Young. "No More Fomo: Limiting Social Media Decreases Loneliness and Depression." *Journal of Social and Clinical Psychology* 370, no. 10 (2018):751–68. https://doi.org/10.1521/jscp.2018.37.10.751

33. Goldstein, Rita Z., and Nora D. Volkow. "Dysfunction of the Prefrontal Cortex in Addiction: Neuroimaging Findings and Clinical Implications." *Nature Reviews Neuroscience* 12, no. 11 (2011):652–69. https://doi.org/10.1038/nrn3119

34. Gupta, Nidhi. "Impact of Smartphone Overuse on Health and Well-Being: Review and Recommendations for Life-Technology Balance." *Journal of Applied Sciences and Clinical Practice* 4, no. 1 (2023):4–12. https://doi.org/10.4103/jascp.jascp_40_22

35. Zadra, Sina, Gallus Bischof, Bettina Besser, Anja Bischof, Christian Meyer, Ulrich John, and Hans-Jürgen Rumpf. "The Association between Internet Addiction and Personality Disorders in a General Population-Based Sample." *Journal of Behavioral Addictions* 5, no. 4 (2016):691–9. https://doi.org/10.1556/2006.5.2016.086

36. Chak, Katherine, and Louis Leung. "Shyness and Locus of Control as Predictors of Internet Addiction and Internet Use." *Cyberpsychology & Behavior* 7, no. 5 (2004):559–70. https://doi.org/10.1089/cpb.2004.7.559

37. Öztürk, Ayfer, and Necla Kundakçı. "Loneliness, Perceived Social Support, and Psychological Resilience as Predictors of Internet Addiction: A Cross-Sectional Study with a Sample of Turkish Undergraduates." *Psychiatry and Clinical Psychopharmacology* 31, no. 4 (2021):449–56. https://doi.org/10.5152/pcp.2021.21115

38. Zhang, Shujie, Yu Tian, Yi Sui, Denghao Zhang, Jieru Shi, Peng Wang, Weixuan Meng, and Yingdong Si. "Relationships between Social Support, Loneliness, and Internet Addiction in Chinese Postsecondary Students: A Longitudinal Cross-Lagged Analysis." *Frontiers in Psychology* 9 (2018):1707. https://doi.org/10.3389/fpsyg.2018.01707

39. Liang, Licha, Dan Zhou, Chunyong Yuan, Aihui Shao, and Yufang Bian. "Gender Differences in the Relationship between Internet Addiction and Depression: A Cross-Lagged Study in Chinese Adolescents." *Computers in Human Behavior* 63 (2016):463–70. https://doi.org/10.1016/j.chb.2016.04.043

40. Becker, Jill B., and Elena Chartoff. "Sex Differences in Neural Mechanisms Mediating Reward and Addiction." *Neuropsychopharmacology* 44, no. 1 (2019):166–83. https://doi.org/10.1038/s41386-018-0125-6

41. Bianchi, Adriana, and James G. Phillips. "Psychological Predictors of Problem Mobile Phone Use." *Cyberpsychology & Behavior* 8, no. 1 (2005):39–51. https://doi.org/10.1089/cpb.2005.8.39

42. Lopez-Fernandez, Olatz, Luisa Honrubia-Serrano, Montserrat Freixa-Blanxart, and Will Gibson. "Prevalence of Problematic Mobile Phone Use in British Adolescents." *Cyberpsychology, Behavior, and Social Networking* 17, no. 2 (2014):91–8. https://doi.org/10.1089/cyber.2012.0260

43. Ahmed, Ishfaq, Tehmina Fiaz Qazi, and Khadija Aijaz Perji. "Mobile Phone to Youngsters: Necessity or Addiction." *African Journal of Business Management* 5, no. 32 (2011):12512–9. https://doi.org/10.5897/AJBM11.626

44. Sahin, Sevil, Kevser Ozdemir, Alaattin Unsal, and Nazen Temiz. "Evaluation of Mobile Phone Addiction Level and Sleep Quality in University Students." *Pak J Med Sci* 29, no. 4 (2013):913–8. https://doi.org/10.12669/pjms.294.3686

45. Christodoulou, Georgia, Anuja Majmundar, Chih-Ping Chou, and Mary A. Pentz. "Anhedonia, Screen Time, and Substance Use in Early Adolescents: A Longitudinal Mediation Analysis." *Journal of Adolescence* 78 (2020):24–32. https://doi.org/10.1016/j.adolescence.2019.11.007

46. Haubursin, Christophe. "It's Not You. Phones are Designed to be Addicting." *Vox* February 27, 2018. https://www.vox.com/2018/2/27/17053758/phone-addictive-design-google-apple

47. Addiction Center. "Phone Addiction. Warning Signs and Treatment." January 29, 2025. https://www.addictioncenter.com/behavioral-addictions/phone-addiction/

48. De-Sola, José, Hernán Talledo, Gabriel Rubio, and Fernando Rodriguez de Fonseca. "Development of a Mobile Phone Addiction Craving Scale and Its Validation in a Spanish Adult Population." *Frontiers in Psychiatry* 8 (2017):90. https://doi.org/10.3389/fpsyt.2017.00090

49. Koo, Hyun Y. "[Development of a Cell Phone Addiction Scale for Korean Adolescents]." *Journal of the Korean Academy of Nursing* 39, no. 6 (2009):818–28. https://doi.org/10.4040/jkan.2009.39.6.818

50. Kwon, Min, Dai-Jin Kim, Hyun Cho, and Soo Yang. "The Smartphone Addiction Scale: Development and Validation of a Short Version for Adolescents." *PLoS ONE* 8, no. 12 (2013):e83558. https://doi.org/10.1371/journal.pone.0083558

51. Lopez-Fernandez, Olatz. "Short Version of the Smartphone Addiction Scale Adapted to Spanish and French: Towards a Cross-Cultural Research in Problematic Mobile Phone Use." *Addictive Behaviors* 64 (2017):275–80. https://doi.org/10.1016/j.addbeh.2015.11.013

52. Lin, Yu-Hsuan, Li-Ren Chang, Yang-Han Lee, Hsien-Wei Tseng, Terry B. J. Kuo, and Sue-Huei Chen. "Development and Validation of the Smartphone Addiction Inventory (Spai)." *PLoS ONE* 9, no. 6 (2014):e98312. https://doi.org/10.1371/journal.pone.0098312

53. Khoury, Julia M., André A. C. de Freitas, Marco A. V. Roque, Maicon R. Albuquerque, Maila C. L. das Neves, and Frederico D. Garcia. "Assessment of the Accuracy of a New Tool for the Screening of Smartphone Addiction." *PLoS ONE* 12, no. 5 (2017):e0176924. https://doi.org/10.1371/journal.pone.0176924

54. Venkatesh, Elluru, Mohammad Y. A. Jemal, and Abdullah S. A. Samani. "Smart Phone Usage and Addiction among Dental Students in Saudi Arabia: A Cross Sectional Study." *International Journal of Adolescent Medicine and Health* 31, no. 1 (2017):20160133. https://doi.org/10.1515/ijamh-2016-0133

55. Basu, Suarav, Suneela Garg, M. Meghachandra Singh, and Charu Kohli. "Addiction-Like Behavior Associated with Mobile Phone Usage among Medical Students in Delhi." *Indian Journal of Psychological Medicine* 40, no. 5 (2018):446–51. https://doi.org/10.4103/IJPSYM.IJPSYM_59_18

56. Chin, Fung, and Chi Hung Leung. "The Concurrent Validity of the Internet Addiction Test (Iat) and the Mobile Phone Dependence Questionnaire (Mpdq)." *PLoS ONE* 13, no. 6 (2018):e0197562. https://doi.org/10.1371/journal.pone.0197562

57. Daei, Azra, Hasan Ashrafi-Rizi, and Mohammad R. Soleymani. "Nomophobia and Health Hazards: Smartphone Use and Addiction among University Students." *International Journal of Preventive Medicine* 10 (2019):202. https://doi.org/10.4103/ijpvm.IJPVM_184_19

58. Lu, Li, Dan-Dan Xu, Huan-Zhong Liu, Ling Zhang, Chee H. Ng, Gabor S. Ungvari, Weng T. Wu, Yi-Fan Xiang, Feng-Rong An, and Yu-Tao Xiang. "Mobile Phone Addiction in Tibetan and Han Chinese Adolescents." *Perspectives in Psychiatric Care* 55, no. 3 (2019):438–44. https://doi.org/10.1111/ppc.12336

59. King, Anna L., Alexandre M. Valenca, and Antonio E. Nardi. "Nomophobia: The Mobile Phone in Panic Disorder with Agoraphobia: Reducing Phobias or Worsening of Dependence?" *Cognitive and Behavioral Neurology* 23, no. 1 (2010):52–4. https://doi.org/10.1097/WNN.0b013e3181b7eabc

60. King, Anna L., Alexandre M. Valenca, Adriana C. Silva, Federica Sancassiani, Sergio Machado, and Antonio E. Nardi. " 'Nomophobia': Impact of Cell Phone Use Interfering with Symptoms and Emotions of Individuals with Panic Disorder Compared with a Control Group." *Clinical Practice and Epidemiology in Mental Health* 10 (2014):28–35. https://doi.org/10.2174/1745017901410010028

61. Sisson, Susan B., Stephanie T. Broyles, Birgitta L. Baker, and Peter T. Katzmarzyk. "Screen Time, Physical Activity, and Overweight in U.S. Youth: National Survey of Children's Health 2003." *The Journal of Adolescent Health* 47, no. 3 (2010):309–11. https://doi.org/10.1016/j.jadohealth.2010.02.016

62. Börnhorst, Claudia, Trudy M. A. Wijnhoven, Marie Kunešová, Agneta Yngve, Ana I. Rito, Lauren Lissner, Vesselka Duleva, Ausra Petrauskiene, and João Breda. "Who European Childhood Obesity Surveillance Initiative: Associations between Sleep Duration, Screen Time and Food Consumption Frequencies." *BMC Public Health* 15 (2015):442. https://doi.org/10.1186/s12889-015-1793-3

63. Temple, Jennifer L., April M. Giacomelli, Kristine M. Kent, James N. Roemmich, and Leonard H. Epstein. "Television Watching Increases Motivated Responding for Food and Energy Intake in Children." *The American Journal of Clinical Nutrition* 85, no. 2 (2007):355–61. https://doi.org/10.1093/ajcn/85.2.355

64. Chaput, Jean-Philippe, Trine Visby, Signe Nyby, Lars Klingenberg, Nikolaj T. Gregersen, Angelo Tremblay, Arne Astrup, and Anders Sjödin. "Video Game Playing Increases Food Intake in Adolescents: A Randomized Crossover Study." *The American Journal of Clinical Nutrition* 93, no. 6 (2011):1196–203. https://doi.org/10.3945/ajcn.110.008680

65. Bel-Serrat, Silvia, Ana Ojeda-Rodriguez, Mirjam M. Heinen, Marta Buoncristiano, Shynar Abdrakhmanova, Vesselka Duleva, Victoria Farrugia Sant'Angelo, et al. "Clustering of Multiple Energy Balance–Related Behaviors in School Children and Its Association with Overweight and Obesity–WHO European Childhood Obesity Surveillance Initiative (Cosi 2015(-)2017)." *Nutrients* 11, no. 3 (2019):511. https://doi.org/10.3390/nu11030511

66. Rosen, L. D., A. F. Lim, J. Felt, L. M. Carrier, N. A. Cheever, J. M. Lara-Ruiz, J. S. Mendoza, and J. Rokkum. "Media and Technology Use Predicts Ill-Being among Children, Preteens and Teenagers Independent of the Negative Health Impacts of Exercise and Eating Habits." *Computers in Human Behavior* 35 (2014):364–75. https://doi.org/10.1016/j.chb.2014.01.036

67. Zhang, Meng X., and Anise M. S. Wu. "Effects of Smartphone Addiction on Sleep Quality among Chinese University Students: The Mediating Role of Self-Regulation and Bedtime Procrastination." *Addictive Behaviors* 111 (2020):106552. https://doi.org/10.1016/j.addbeh.2020.106552

68. Gradisar, Michael, Amy R. Wolfson, Allison G. Harvey, Lauren Hale, Russell Rosenberg, and Charles A. Czeisler. "The Sleep and Technology Use of Americans: Findings from the National Sleep Foundation's 2011 Sleep in America Poll." *Journal of Clinical Sleep Medicine* 9, no. 12 (2013):1291–9. https://doi.org/10.5664/jcsm.3272

69. Sletten, Tracey L., Victoria L. Revell, Benita Middleton, Katharin A. Lederle, and Debra J. Skene. "Age-Related Changes in Acute and Phase-Advancing Responses to Monochromatic Light." *Journal of Biological Rhythms* 24, no. 1 (2009):73–84. https://doi.org/10.1177/0748730408328973

70. Margrain, T. H., M. Boulton, J. Marshall, and D. H. Sliney. "Do Blue Light Filters Confer Protection against Age-Related Macular Degeneration?" *Progress in Retinal and Eye Research* 23, no. 5 (2004):523–31. https://doi.org/10.1016/j.preteyeres.2004.05.001

71. Hong, Wei, Ru-De Liu, Yi Ding, Xiaotian Sheng, and Rui Zhen. "Mobile Phone Addiction and Cognitive Failures in Daily Life: The Mediating Roles of Sleep Duration and Quality and the Moderating Role of Trait Self-Regulation." *Addictive Behaviors* 107 (2020):106383. https://doi.org/10.1016/j.addbeh.2020.106383

72. Falbe, Jennifer, Kirsten K. Davison, Rebecca L. Franckle, Claudia Ganter, Steven L. Gortmaker, Lauren Smith, Thomas Land, and Elsie M. Taveras. "Sleep Duration, Restfulness, and Screens in the Sleep Environment." *Pediatrics* 135, no. 2 (2015):e367-75. https://doi.org/10.1542/peds.2014-2306

73. Arora, T., S. Hussain, K. B. Hubert Lam, G. Lily Yao, G. Neil Thomas, and S. Taheri. "Exploring the Complex Pathways among Specific Types of Technology, Self-Reported Sleep Duration and Body Mass Index in UK Adolescents." *International Journal of Obesity* 37, no. 9 (2013):1254–60. https://doi.org/10.1038/ijo.2012.209

74. Calamaro, Christina J., Kyeongra Yang, Sarah Ratcliffe, and Eileen R. Chasens. "Wired at a Young Age: The Effect of Caffeine and Technology on Sleep Duration and Body Mass Index in School-Aged Children." *Journal of Pediatric Health Care* 26, no. 4 (2012):276–82. https://doi.org/10.1016/j.pedhc.2010.12.002

75. Martin, Michelle. Computer and Internet Use in the United States: 2018. United States Census Bureau,; 2021. Contract No.: ACS-49.

76. Grontved, Anders, John Singhammer, Karsten Froberg, Niels C. Moller, An Pan, Karin A. Pfeiffer, and Peter L. Kristensen. "A Prospective Study of Screen Time in Adolescence and Depression Symptoms in Young Adulthood." *Preventive Medicine* 81 (2015):108–13. https://doi.org/10.1016/j.ypmed.2015.08.009

77. Nigg, Claudio R., Kathrin Wunsch, Carina Nigg, Claudia Niessner, Darko Jekauc, Steffen C. E. Schmidt, and Alexander Woll. "Is Physical Activity, Screen Time, and Mental Health Related During Childhood, Preadolescence, and Adolescence? 11-Year Results from the German Momo Cohort Trial." *American Journal of Epidemiology* 190, no. 2 (2021):220–9. https://doi.org/10.1093/aje/kwaa192

78. Liu, Jianghong, Susan Riesch, Joyce Tien, Terri Lipman, Jennifer Pinto-Martin, and Ann O'Sullivan. "Screen Media Overuse and Associated Physical, Cognitive, and Emotional/Behavioral Outcomes in Children and Adolescents: An Integrative Review." *Journal of Pediatric Health Care* 36, no. 2 (2022):99–109. https://doi.org/10.1016/j.pedhc.2021.06.003

79. Braig, Stefanie, Jon Genuneit, Viola Walter, Stephanie Brandt, Martin Wabitsch, Lutz Goldbeck, Hermann Brenner, and Dietrich Rothenbacher. "Screen Time, Physical Activity and Self-Esteem in Children: The Ulm Birth Cohort Study." *International Journal of Environmental Research and Public Health* 15, no. 6 (2018):1275. https://doi.org/10.3390/ijerph15061275

80. Feng, Qi, Qing-le Zhang, Yue Du, Yong-ling Ye, and Qi-qiang He. "Associations of Physical Activity, Screen Time with Depression, Anxiety and Sleep Quality among Chinese College Freshmen." *PLoS ONE* 9, no. 6 (2014):e100914. https://doi.org/10.1371/journal.pone.0100914

81. Kushlev, Kostadin, Jason D. E. Proulx, and Elizabeth W. Dunn. "Digitally Connected, Socially Disconnected: The Effects of Relying on Technology Rather Than Other People." *Computers in Human Behavior* 76 (2017):68–74. https://doi.org/10.1016/j.chb.2017.07.001

82. Ivanova, Ana, Oleg Gorbaniuk, Aagata Blachnio, Aneta Przepiorka, Natalia Mraka, Viktoria Polishchuk, and Julia Gorbaniuk. "Mobile Phone Addiction, Phubbing, and Depression among Men and Women: A Moderated Mediation Analysis." *The Psychiatric Quarterly* 91, no. 3 (2020):655–68. https://doi.org/10.1007/s11126-020-09723-8

83. Satici, Seydi Ahmet, and Recep Uysal. "Well-Being and Problematic Facebook Use." *Computers in Human Behavior* 49 (2015):185–90. https://doi.org/10.1016/j.chb.2015.03.005

84. Twenge, Jean M., Zlatan Krizan, and Garrett Hisler. "Decreases in Self-Reported Sleep Duration among U.S. Adolescents 2009–2015 and Association with New Media Screen Time." *Sleep Medicine* 39 (2017):47–53. https://doi.org/10.1016/j.sleep.2017.08.013

85. Heijnen, Saskia, Bernhard Hommel, Armin Kibele, and Lorenza S. Colzato. "Neuromodulation of Aerobic Exercise-A Review." *Frontiers in Psychology* 6 (2016):1890. https://doi.org/10.3389/fpsyg.2015.01890

86. Wang, Jin-Liang, Hai-Zhen Wang, James Gaskin, and Skyler Hawk. "The Mediating Roles of Upward Social Comparison and Self-Esteem and the Moderating Role of Social Comparison Orientation in the Association between Social Networking Site Usage and Subjective Well-Being." *Frontiers in Psychology* 8 (2017):771. https://doi.org/10.3389/fpsyg.2017.00771

87. Feng, Wenting, Dihui Chang, and Hongjie Sun. "The impact of social media influencers' bragging language styles on consumers' attitudes toward luxury brands: The dual mediation of envy and trustworthiness." *Frontiers in Psychology* 13 (2023): 1113655.

88. Pariser, Eli. *The Filter Bubble: What the Internet Is Hiding from You:* Penguin Press, 2011.

89. Twenge, Jean M., and W. Keith Campbell. "Associations between Screen Time and Lower Psychological Well-Being among Children and Adolescents: Evidence from a Population-Based Study." *Preventive Medicine* Reports 12 (2018):271–83. https://doi.org/10.1016/j.pmedr.2018.10.003

90. Leventhal, Adam M., Junhan Cho, Katherine M. Keyes, Jennifer Zink, Kira E. Riehm, Yi Zhang, and Elizabeth Ketema. "Digital Media Use and Suicidal Behavior in U.S. Adolescents, 2009–2017." *Preventive Medicine Reports* 23 (2021):101497. https://doi.org/10.1016/j.pmedr.2021.101497

91. Carson, Valerie, William Pickett, and Ian Janssen. "Screen Time and Risk Behaviors in 10- to 16-Year-Old Canadian Youth." *Preventive Medicine* 52, no. 2 (2011):99–103. https://doi.org/10.1016/j.ypmed.2010.07.005

92. Onyeaka, Henry K., Chioma Muoghalu, Philip Baiden, Lucinda Okine, Hannah S. Szlyk, JaNiene E. Peoples, Erin Kasson, Patricia Cavazos-Rehg, Joseph Firth, and John Torous. Excessive screen time behaviors and cognitive difficulties among adolescents in the United States: Results from the 2017 and 2019 national youth risk behavior survey. *Psychiatry Research* 316(2022):114740. https://doi.org/10.1016/j.psychres.2022.114740

93. Mark, Gloria, Victor M. Gonzalez, and Justin Harris. "No Task Left Behind? Examining the Nature of Fragmented Work." *In: Proceedings of the Special Interest Group on Computer-Human Interaction (SIGCHI) Conference on Human Factors in Computing Systems,* Portland, Oregon, USA (2005): 321–30. https://doi.org/10.1145/1054972.1055017

94. Shelton, Jill T., Emily M. Elliott, Sharon D. Lynn, and Amanda L. Exner. "The Distracting Effects of a Ringing Cell Phone: An Investigation of the Laboratory and the Classroom Setting." *J Environ Psychol* 29, no. 4 (2009):513–21. https://doi.org/10.1016/j.jenvp.2009.03.001

95. Wulfhorst, Ellen. U.S. Worker Interruptions Costly, Research Shows. Reuters. 2007 August 9.

96. Gill, Preetinder S., Ashwini Kamath, and Tejkaran S. Gill. "Distraction: An Assessment of Smartphone Usage in Health Care Work Settings." *Risk Management and Healthcare Policy* 5 (2012):105–14. https://doi.org/10.2147/RMHP.S34813

97. Hoppel, Ann M. "Smartphones and Dumb Behavior." Clinician Reviews 22, no. 2 (2012):C1, 21–3.

98. Smith, T, E Darling, and B Searles. "2010 Survey on Cell Phone Use While Performing Cardiopulmonary Bypass." *Perfusion* 26, no. 5 (2011):375–80. https://doi.org/10.1177/0267659111409969

99. McBride, Deborah L. "The Distracted Nurse." *Journal of Pediatric Nursing* 27, no. 3 (2012):275–6. https://doi.org/10.1016/j.pedn.2012.02.002

100. Rosenfield, Daniel, Paul C. Hébert, Matthew B. Stanbrook, Noni E. MacDonald, and Ken Flegel. "Being Smarter with Smartphones." *Canadian Medical Association Journal* 183, no. 18 (2011):E1276. https://doi.org/10.1503/cmaj.110524

101. Katz-Sidlow, Rachel J., Allison Ludwig, Scott Miller, and Robert Sidlow. "Smartphone Use During Inpatient Attending Rounds: Prevalence, Patterns and Potential for Distraction." *Journal of Hospital Medicine* 7, no. 8 (2012):595–9. https://doi.org/10.1002/jhm.1950

102. Drummond, Dike. *Stop Physician Burnout: What to Do When Working Harder Isn't Working:* Heritage Press Publications, LLC, 2014.

103. Dingus, Thomas A., Feng Guo, Suzie Lee, Jonathan F. Antin, Miguel Perez, Mindy Buchanan-King, and Jonathan Hankey. "Driver Crash Risk Factors and Prevalence Evaluation Using Naturalistic Driving Data." *Proceedings of the National Academy of Sciences* 113, no. 10 (2016):2636–41. https://doi.org/10.1073/pnas.1513271113

104. McNabb, Jaimie, and Rob Gray. "Staying Connected on the Road: A Comparison of Different Types of Smart Phone Use in a Driving Simulator." *PLoS ONE* 11, no. 2 (2016):e0148555. https://doi.org/10.1371/journal.pone.0148555

105. Caird, Jeff K., Kate A. Johnston, Chelsea R. Willness, Mark Asbridge, and Piers Steel. "A Meta-Analysis of the Effects of Texting on Driving." *Accident Analysis & Prevention* 71 (2014):311–8. https://doi.org/10.1016/j.aap.2014.06.005

106. Caird, Jeff K., Chelsea R. Willness, Piers Steel, and Chip Scialfa. "A Meta-Analysis of the Effects of Cell Phones on Driver Performance." *Accident Analysis & Prevention* 40, no. 4 (2008):1282–93. https://doi.org/10.1016/j.aap.2008.01.009

107. Horberry, Tim, Janet Anderson, Michael A. Regan, Thomas J. Triggs, and John Brown. "Driver Distraction: The Effects of Concurrent in-Vehicle Tasks, Road Environment Complexity and Age on Driving Performance." *Accident Analysis & Prevention* 38, no. 1 (2006):185–91. https://doi.org/10.1016/j.aap.2005.09.007

108. McCartt, Anne T., Laurie A. Hellinga, and Keli A. Bratiman. "Cell Phones and Driving: Review of Research." *Traffic Injury Prevention* 7, no. 2 (2006):89–106. https://doi.org/10.1080/15389580600651103

109. Zendrive. "2018 Snapshot: Distracted Driving Is 100x Worse Than Thought." Zendrive. Last modified 2018. https://www.zendrive.com/data-studies/2018-distracted-driving-snapshot-distracted-driving-is-100-times-worse-than-thought

110. National Highway Traffic Safety Administration. "Distracted Driving." U.S. Department of Transportation. Last modified 2023. https://www.nhtsa.gov/risky-driving/distracted-driving

111. AAA Foundation for Traffic Safety. "2017 Traffic Safety Culture Index." Last modified 2018. http://aaafoundation.org/wp-content/uploads/2018/03/TSCI-2017-Report.pdf

112. Nelson, Erik, Paul Atchley, and Todd D. Little. "The Effects of Perception of Risk and Importance of Answering and Initiating a Cellular Phone Call While Driving." *Accident Analysis & Prevention* 41, no. 3 (2009):438–44. https://doi.org/10.1016/j.aap.2009.01.006

113. Nemme, Heidi E., and Katherine M. White. "Texting While Driving: Psychosocial Influences on Young People's Texting Intentions and Behaviour." *Accident Analysis & Prevention* 42, no. 4 (2010):1257–65. https://doi.org/10.1016/j.aap.2010.01.019

114. Yeo, Jiho, and Shin-Hyoung Park. "Effect of Smartphone Dependency on Smartphone Use While Driving." *Sustainability* 13, no. 10 (2021):5604. https://doi.org/10.3390/su13105604

115. Valero-Mora, Pedro M., Juan J. Zacarés, Mar Sánchez-García, Maria T. Tormo-Lancero, and Mireia Faus. "Conspiracy Beliefs Are Related to the Use of Smartphones Behind the Wheel." *International Journal of Environmental Research and Public Health* 18, no. 15 (2021):7725. https://doi.org/10.3390/ijerph18157725

116. Young, Kristie L., Christina M. Rudin-Brown, Christopher Patten, Ruggero Ceci, and Michael G. Lenné. "Effects of Phone Type on Driving and Eye Glance Behaviour While Text-Messaging." *Safety Science* 68 (2014):47–54. https://doi.org/10.1016/j.ssci.2014.02.018

117. Hatfield, Julie, and Susanne Murphy. "The Effects of Mobile Phone Use on Pedestrian Crossing Behaviour at Signalized and Unsignalized Intersections." *Accident Analysis & Prevention* 39, no. 1 (2007):197–205. https://doi.org/10.1016/j.aap.2006.07.001

118. Virginia Tech Transportation Institution. "Distracted Driving Awareness." Last modified 2024. https://www.vtti.vt.edu/projects/distracted-driving.html

119. Council on Communications and Media. "Media Use in School-Aged Children and Adolescents." *Pediatrics* 138, no. 5 (2016):e20162592. https://doi.org/10.1542/peds.2016-2592

120. Council on Communications and Media. "Media and Young Minds." *Pediatrics* 138, no. 5 (2016):e20162591. https://doi.org/10.1542/peds.2016-2591

121. Goh, Si Ning, Long Hua Teh, Wei Rong Tay, Saradha Anantharaman, Rob M. van Dam, Chuen Seng Tan, Hwee Ling Chua, Pey Gein Wong, and Falk Müller-Riemenschneider. "Sociodemographic, Home Environment and Parental Influences on Total and Device-Specific Screen Viewing in Children Aged 2 Years and Below: An Observational Study." *BMJ Open* 6, no. 1 (2016):e009113. https://doi.org/10.1136/bmjopen-2015-009113

122. Real, Terrence. *I Don't Want to Talk About It: Overcoming the Secret Legacy of Male Depression:* Simon and Schuster, 1997.

123. Plummer, Matt. "How to Spend Way Less Time on Email Every Day." *Harvard Business Review.* January 22, 2019. https://hbr.org/2019/01/how-to-spend-way-less-time-on-email-every-day

124. Once, Liezel. "Gen Z stressed by email overload at work – Babbel survey." May 9, 2024. https://news.outsourceaccelerator.com/gen-z-stressed-email-babbel/

Index

About the Author

Dr. Nidhi Gupta is a pediatric endocrinologist, TEDx speaker, and internationally recognized expert on digital wellness. An award-winning researcher with over 100 publications, she is the founder of the Phreedom Foundation, a nonprofit committed to helping people reclaim their time, attention, and joy in an increasingly distracted world.

Her work began in 2014, when personal and clinical experiences prompted her to explore the growing relationship between humans and their devices. She observed a troubling paradox: while we're more digitally connected than ever, we're also more disconnected from ourselves and each other.

In response, Dr. Gupta launched the Phreedom Foundation (Ungrip Devices. Grip Life) in 2019, dedicated to helping individuals, families, and professionals create healthier relationships with technology, not just by reducing screen time, but by reawakening purpose and presence in everyday life.

Her research has linked digital overuse to anxiety, sleep disruption, burnout, obesity, and fragmented attention, making her a trusted voice in the global conversation on tech and health. Through retreats, coaching, school partnerships, and corporate workshops, she has inspired a growing movement toward intentional living.

Calm the Noise is the natural extension of her mission. It is a personal and scientific guide to leading by example in the digital age.

www.ingramcontent.com/pod-product-compliance
Lightning Source LLC
Chambersburg PA
CBHW021143130626
46554CB00005B/1643